CLOCK AND WATCH MAKERS

OF

ABERDEEN AND NORTH EAST SCOTLAND

1453 – 1900

Donald Whyte
FHG, FSG (HON.)

CONTENTS

Preface v

Clock and Watch Makers 1

Addenda and Time Periods 43

Principal sources 44

Abbreviations 46

County abbreviations 47

Illustrations

Front cover: samples of watch-papers

Notice of removal 48

Dedicated to the late

FELIX HUDSON

Horologist, Dunfermline

PREFACE

My little work, *Scottish Clock and Watch Makers*, published by the Scottish Genealogy Society in 1996, provided a useful checklist of Scottish makers, giving their names, working dates (as far as found), and where possible what they actually did, apart from clock and watch making. However, a reviewer tritely remarked that readers would "inevitably be left wanting more".

To produce a comprehensive work covering all Scotland would require a large volume, perhaps two, and it would not be easy to find a publisher for what might be considered a 'minority interest'. Only John Smith's pioneer work, *Old Scottish Clockmakers, 1453 to 1850*, a 2nd edition of which was published by Oliver & Boyd, of Edinburgh, in 1921 (reprinted by EP Publishing at Wakefield in 1975, without revision or enlargement), attempted to cover the whole country. It is extremely doubtful if he listed half of the clock and watch makers, but with nothing with which to compare his book, it has been described as "a classic".

More recent works with a national theme include the late Felix Hudson's pamphlet, *Scottish Clockmakers: A Brief History up to 1900* (Dunfermline, 1984), but that was not an attempt to list the craftsmen. *500 Years of Scottish Clockmaking*, by Mich Dareau (Edinburgh, 1997), is a catalogue of items displayed at an exhibition held at Callendar House, Falkirk. This work gives valuable technical information. A more full catalogue is promised.

It seems that treatment by individual towns and / or districts is most feasible. *The Aberdeen Journal*, in 1921-22, published a long series of articles, mainly about clock and watch makers in the North-East. In 1981 William Wallace printed a useful pamphlet, *Marking Time in Hamilton*. The most notable contribution is *Dunfermline Clockmakers*, by Jean and Martin Norgate, and Felix Hudson (Dunfermline, 1982). This model study may have inspired Charles Allan, whose well-researched book, *Old Stirling Clockmakers*, was published in 1990. The present work covers North-East Scotland: the old counties of Aberdeenshire, Kincardineshire and Banffshire, as those areas were understood previous to the 1975 re-organisation of local government, and in the records held by the Registrar General for Scotland covering the years treated in this work.

Lads who were apprenticed to clock and watchmakers had to be prepared for a spartan existence. They were usually apprenticed for 6 or 7 years, and to become journeymen had to demonstrate their hard won skills by producing an example of their work, called an 'essay'. If they passed they were admitted to the Incorporation of Hammermen, which in each town of any size, governed all workers in metal. Very often they commenced business on their own account and were admitted as trade burgesses.

A useful source of information about clock and watchmakers is the roundels or watchpapers which the craftsmen inserted in the backs of pocket watches. The original purpose was probably to protect or cushion the gold or silver backs, and to prevent dust from entering the keyholes, but the watchpapers also served the same purpose of modern business cards. The practice appears to have begun in London, and became common in Scotland around 1780. At first these gave only the names and addresses of makers, but gradually borders were used to advertise not only clocks and watches but other services such as engraving and silver plating, and items such as cutlery, barometers and musical boxes. As street directories – where these exist – lump the craftsmen under CLOCK AND WATCHMAKERS, or WATCHMAKERS AND JEWELLERS, leaving a lot unsaid, the watchpapers tell us much more about their activities. I am indebted to several collectors for copies of watchpapers, notably the late Felix Hudson, of Dunfermline and David M. Penney, a former editor of *Antiquarian Horology*, who also generously provided copies of billheads, another source of information. Thanks are also due to the Local Studies Department of Aberdeen Central Public Library, for a xerox copy of R. Murdoch Lawrance's *Notes on the Old Clockmakers*, which appeared in the Aberdeen Journal, 1921/22. For editorial assistance I am indebted to Mrs Jean Shirer, of the Publications Sub-Committee of the Aberdeen & North-East Scotland Family History Society.

In the interests of economy, abbreviations are used in this work, mainly for the trades undertaken, e.g. WM & J, for watchmaker and jeweller. Also shortened are the names of Scottish counties. The abbreviations are given at pp. 46 and 47. Cross-references to makers in entries, are indicated in capital letters, but not bold. No claims to completeness are made for this book, but it should be of assistance to collectors, auctioneers, clock restorers, museums, libraries, record offices, horological writers, historians and especially genealogists.

DONALD WHYTE

4 Carmel Road
Kirkliston
EH29 9DD

CLOCK & WATCH MAKERS
OF
ABERDEEN & NORTH- EAST SCOTLAND

ABEL, WILLIAM. Banff, ca. 1870. Poss. succ. by J. INVERARITY. Wpr.- of Mid Victorian design: WILLIAM ABEL / [Burgh arms] / WATCHMAKER & JEWELLER / 35 LOW STREET, BANFF. Fml. bdr.

ABERCROMBIE, JAMES. In business in Aberdeen as C & WM before 1730. Deacon of the Inc. of Hmm. there, 1734-38, 1750-51, and alive 1757. Witnessed baptisms at St. Paul's Episcopal Church from 1730 onwards. Ensign in the town Volunteers, 1748.

ADAM, WILLIAM. WM in BANFF, ca. 1840. Wpr.- Wm. ADAM / CERTIFICATED / WATCHMAKER / BANFF, NB. Str. & bkl. bdr.

ADAMS, GEORGE. Old Meldrum, ABD, ca. 1880. Wpr.- GEORGE ADAMS / WATCH MAKER / OLD MELDRUM. Str. & bkl. bdr., advertising repairs.

ADAMS, J. WM & J, 2D Thistle Street, Aberdeen, 1899-1900+.

AITKEN, JAMES. C & WM, Kincardine O'Neil, ABD, ca. 1827-47.

AITKEN, WILLIAM. C & WM, Auchinblae, ABD, ca. 1860.

ALEXANDER, GEORGE. C & WM, Turriff, ABD, 1838-50. He was s/o JAMES A., to whose business he succeeded after 1838.

ALEXANDER, JAMES. C & WM, Turriff, ABD, 1828-35. He m. 7.12.1828, Mary Sheriffs. Chrn: 1. James, b. 1829; 2. GEORGE, b. 1830, succ. to his father's business; 3. Robert, b. 1832; 4. William, b. 1834. George, Sr., d. 20.3.1835, aged 39 years. His widow carried on the business until son GEORGE was old enough to take over.

ALEXANDER, JAMES. WM in Aberdeen, 1840-50, perhaps a jour. He resided at Hutcheon Street. Had several chrn, who dy. He d. 3.11.1850, aged 50 years.

ALEXANDER, JAMES. At Schoolhill, Aberdeen, 1855. By 1860 at 6 Union Street. Moved to No.113, where in business until ca. 1888. Wpr.- JAS. ALEXANDER / WATCH / AND / CLOCK MAKER / 6 UNION STREET / ABERDEEN. Orn. bdr. His daughter Mary Walker A., m. George Mennie, sometime of Aberdeen, and d. at Johannesburg, SA, 21.8.1892.

ALEXANDER, JAMES. C & WM, Kincardine O'Neil, ABD, ca. 1846.

ALEXANDER, W. C & WM, Bucksburn, ABD, ca. 1810.

ALLAN, COLIN. CM, GLS & J, Foot o' Dee, Aberdeen, 1748-1800. Adm. to the Inc. of Hmm of Aberdeen, 5.10.1748, and was Deacon in 1761, 1763, 1764 and 1767. Adm. B of Old Aberdeen, 9.1.1762. Deacon of the Inc. Trades, 1763- 64. Colin was a pioneer in the granite polishing industry, making table- tops and gravestones. The trade suffered a relapse, but revived ca. 1820. This versatile craftsman m. Anne, d/o Alexander Irvine of Pitmuxton, and Isobel Duncan. Chrn: 1. Colin, bapt. 18.6.1767, dy; 2. James, attended Marischal College, 1772-73; 3. Helen, bapt. 18.2.1766; 4. Sarah, b. 21.6. 1769; 5. Colin (ii) b. 15.10.1772, graduated MA at Marischal College, and became a physician in Aberdeen. The degree of MD was conferred on him, and he joined the 7th West India Regiment, Hill Forces, 1826. He m. 5.4.1820, Jane Gibbon Knox, and had issue. He d. at Frederickton, NB, 15.5.1850, then on half-pay. His testament was confirmed at Edinburgh.

ALLAN, C.G. In business in Aberdeen, ca. 1865. Wpr.- C.G. ALLAN / PRACTICAL / WATCH & CLOCK / MAKER / 65 / COMMERCE STREET / ABERDEEN. Str. & bkl. bdr., advertising repairs.

ALLAN, JAMES. Cabinet-maker, Aberdeen, from 1818, known to have made clock cases. Became James A. & Sons, cabinet-makers, 122 Union Street, with a manufactory at 42 Dee Street.

ALLAN, JAMES. C & WM, Holborn Street, Aberdeen, 1824-35; at Wellington Place, 1834-37; and at Holborn Place, 1838-56. Resided sometime at 6 Quay, Aberdeen.

ALLAN, JAMES. C & WM, Stonehaven, KCD, 1850-70. By his wife Janet Brown he had chrn: 1. Colin, coppersmith in Aberdeen; 2. Margaret, who d. 26.5. 1855, aged 48; her brother Colin was served heir to her in one quarter of Lot 9, of the lands of Pitmuxton and other subjects, 12.7.1870; 3. Ann.

ALLAN, JOHN. CM in Aberdeen, ca. 1797.

ALLAN, WILLIAM. Appr. to PETER GILL, C & WM, Aberdeen, and prob. in business on his own account by 1790. His only daughter, Margaret, 1779-1852, m. George Mackenzie, 1773-1852, merchant, and was mother of Sir James Thomson Mackenzie, 1818-90, lst Bart. of Glenmuick.

ALLAN, WILLIAM. Appr. to JOHN MEARNS, C & WM, Aberdeen, for 6 years from 18.7.1740, and worked at his trade in Aberdeen from ca. 1747. He was s/o George A., farmer, Mains of Auchingoul, and was alive in 1772.

ANDERSON, ALEXANDER. WM & J, Upperkirkgate, Aberdeen, 1860-69. He was s/o Alexander A., stone-cutter, and Ann Day. He d. aged 33, and was bur. in St. Peter's Chyd., 25.6.1869.

ANDERSON, CHARLES. Aberdeen, 1695. He was adm. a trade-B, 22.3.1699, which caused the Inc. of Hmm. to complain, as he had not been adm. as a freeman of the craft. The Town Council appear to have over-ruled them. He was second s/o John A., merchant-burgess. In the *Poll Tax Returns*, 1695/96, he is described as WM, stock under 500 merks. A brother George resided with him at that time. Charles m. Jean Coutts in 1699.

ANDERSON, GEORGE. C & WM, 36 Green, Aberdeen, 1832-37. He resided at No. 67, and from 1834 at No.65 Green.

ANDERSON, GEORGE. WM & J, 17 Schoolhill, Aberdeen, before 1877. Moved to No.16 by 1886, and at No.18 by 1895. At No.24 in 1900.

ANDERSON, HERCULES. At Bervie, KCD, 1837. Prob. active in the Mid and Late Regency periods. Wpr.- HERcl. ANDERSON / CLOCK AND / WATCH MAKER / BERVIE. Perpetual calender and regulating instructions. On the back "April 1848".

ANDERSON, J. & J.S. WM & J, 7 Back Wynd, Aberdeen, 1873. Moved to 93 Queen Street by 1880; at 96 Rosemount Viaduct by 1890, and at 22 Loch Street by 1900.

ANDERSON, ROBERT. C & WM, Buckie, Banff, 1877.

ANDERSON, WILLIAM. C & WM, Bervie, KCD, 1860-77.

ANDERSON, WILLIAM. Stonehaven, KCD, 1873-1900+. Wpr.- [Royal arms] / Wm. ANDERSON / WATCHMAKER & JEWELLER / 36 MARKET STREET / STONEHAVEN. Orn. bdr. A later wpr. advertises optical services.

ANDERSONE, DAVID. CR, Aberdeen, 1597.

ANDREW, ALEXANDER. C & WM, Portsoy, BAB, 1802-40. Poss. s/o William A., who d. 1807, aged 54 years, and was bur. at Boyndie.

ANDREW, JOHN. C & WM, Huntly, ABD, before 1816. He m. Margaret Wilson. Chrn: 1. George, WM in Arbroath, ANS, 1835-80; 2. WILLIAM.

ANDREW, WILLIAM. Huntly, ABD. Appr. to his father JOHN, 1816, and commenced business on his own account before 1830, at The Square, Huntly. He ret. in 1868, and took up farming at Broomfield, Forgue. William served as a Police Commissionar for many years, and was active as a Freemason for many years, and as a Sabbath School teacher in the Free Church. He m. 1.3.1852, at Fife-Keith, Jessie, d/o Alexander Milne and Jessie Copeland. William d. 19.12.1883. His widow lived to an advanced age, having bore him chrn: 1. Jessie, b. 1852; 2. Clementine, b. 1853; 3. William, emigrated to the USA; 4. Isabella, b. 1864.

ANGUS, GEORGE. Appr. to PETER GILL, C & WM, Aberdeen, for 6 years from 1782. In business Early and Mid Regency periods. The local directory, copy in the Aberdeen Central Public Library, has a marginal note: "Father of the Town Clerk & Mrs Geo. Russel, London". The Town Clerk was John Angus, MA. George built a clock for Union (Shiprow) Church. A longcase clock by him was sold by Christie's Scotland, 14.2.1990. George was a s/o James A., who d. before 1782. He m. Christian Watt, and resided at 4 Drum Lane.

ANTON, WILLIAM A. Huntly, ABD, ca. 1890. Wpr.- Wm. A. ANTON / WATCH-MAKER, JEWELLER / AND OPTICIAN [in MS. No.9323] / 30 DUKE ST. / HUNTLY. Str. & bkl. bdr.

ARGO, JAMES. C & WM, Peterhead, ABD, during the Regency period, and made the first public clock there, preserved in 1921 in the Arbuthnott Museum. In 1834 he is listed as one of the harbour trustees.

AUER, AUGUSTE. German CM, with ptn. PAUL WONDERLY, 1860-72, at 42 George Street, Aberdeen. On his own account at 51 Upperkirkgate, 1872-1900+

B

BANNERMAN, GILBERT. C & WM, Banff, 1764-1812. He appears as a subscriber to *Hymns and Sacred Poems,* by James Fordyce (Aberdeen, 1787). Gilbert m. Anne Smart, who d. 14.8.1814, aged 78 years.

BARRON, JOHN. Appr. to GEORGE MORRISON, C & WM, Aberdeen, for 6 years from 1.11.1780. He was s/o George B., wright, dec. John was adm. to the Inc. of Hmm. of Aberdeen, 26.4.1796, and became a trade-B, 23.10.1797. He was Deacon of the Inc., 1804-12, and lived next door to his shop at 11 Nethergate. Either he or his father was treasurer of the Widows Supplementary Fund of the Inc. Trades, 1847-48. John ret. in 1850, and d. testate, 26.5.1852. He m. Ann Allan, 1773-1837, and had issue: 1. Andrew, 1797-1831, d. at Madras; 2. Janet, 1799-1849; 3. George, 1800-51, W.S., who m. 26.12.1837, Elizabeth, d. 1892, d/o Alexander Adie, optician in Edinburgh; 4. Helen, 1802-10; 5. John, 1804-08; 6. James, 1806-52; 7. JOHN, 1810-47, ptn. with his father, 1832-47; 8. Elizabeth, 1812-58; 9. Ann, 1814-93.

BARRON & SON. The above JOHN B. and his son of the same name, 1832-47, in business at Netherkirkgate, Aberdeen. They built the turret clock of South Parish Church, 1832. Became BARRON & GRAY.

BARRON & GRAY. C & WM, Netherkirkgate, Aberdeen, 1847-48. JOHN B., Jr., and ALEXANDER GRAY.

BEATTIE, JAMES E. WM & J, 13a Correction Wynd, Aberdeen, 1890; at 14 Carmelite Street by 1895.

BERRY, GEORGE ALLAN. C & WM, Aberdeen, 1857-70. Appr. to his father, JAMES B., and became his ptn. in 1857 at 88 Union Street. At 29 St. Nicholas Street, 1861-64. On his own account there, 1864, and at Inverurie by 1870. Subsequently at West Hartlepool, Co. Durham, as WM & J. He had been adm. to the Inc. of Hmm. of Aberdeen, and became a trade-B, 5.2.1866. George m. at London, 6.12.1857, Fanny Bristow, and had issue: 1. George Frank, 1859-1948, WM, who emigrated to Canada; 2. Fanny Christine Eleanor, b. 1850; 3. Annie Isabella, 1864-1945; 4. Eliza, d. inf., 1865; 5. Flora Amelia Evaline, 1870-1956; 6. Alberta Louise Frances, 1871-1964; George Allan B. d. 25.4.1903.

BERRY, JAMES. Commenced business at Stonehaven, KCD, ca. 1835. Moved in 1836 to Aberdeen as CM & J, CRM & NIM, at 52 Castle Street, where in business until 1853. Moved to 88 Union Street, with his son GEORGE ALLAN B. as ptn. until 1864. At 59½ Marischal Street, 1865-66, and became BERRY & MACKAY. He was then residing at 1 Dee Place. James was third s/o James B., shipmaster, and Christine Bissett. He was adm. to the Inc. of Hmm. of Aberdeen, 27.2.1837, and became a trade-B. 10.3.1837. James became a magistrate and a governor of Gordon's College. He also served on the Public Library Committee. Among clocks he erected was one at Crathes Castle, Deeside, and another at Peterhead Parish Church, 1845 and 1850 respectively. He m. Isabella, 1813-1902, d/o George Allan and Jane Bissett. They had issue: 1. GEORGE ALLAN; 2. Jean Allan, b. 1835; 3. William, 1839-1922, who went to South Africa, where he had a distinguished career as a physician and politician, and was knighted; 4. James, resided in Dundee; 5. Christ- ine Helen. 1841-59; 6. Isabella, b. ca. 1844; 7. Eliza Allan, 1846-93; 8. Elsie Milne, 1850-82; 8. Rev. John, 1852-1914, UF Church minister at Ceres, FIF; 9. Andrew Wales, 1854-1915. James d. 19.9.1890.

BERRY & MACKAY. This notable firm commenced in 1879, when Alexander S. Mackay, a skilled optician, joined JAMES BERRY, Aberdeen. He contd. the business after the d. of his ptn. in 1890, and d. at London, 24.7.1914. Detailed information about their instrument making is contained in *Brass & Glass,* published by National Museums of Scotland in 1989.

BISSET, WILLIAM. Alford, ABD, ca. 1860. Wpr.- WILLIAM BISSET / WATCHMAKER / ALFORD. Str. & bkl. bdr. with advert for repairs. A later wpr. shows he was also an optician.

BLACK, JOHN. Foreman with JOHN GARTLY, prob. 1808-22, and poss. for a time with JOHN HARDY. Adm. to the Inc. of Hmm. in 1832, and commenced his own business at Fowler's Wynd before moving to 12 Longacre in 1839. Moved to No.16 before 1840, when listed as CM & OP. He erected a church clock in Fordoun in 1835, under the supervision of JOHN BARRON, another at Old Aberdeen in 1836. A clock he made for Ballater Kirk Session in 1842, was moved to Inverurie in 1879. John m. Isobel Beattie, and d. 24.2.1851, aged 71 years, and was bur. at St. Peter's Chyd, Spittal, Old Aberdeen. Known chrn: 1. Margaret, b. 15.6.1849; 2. Isabella, b. 28.5.1851.

BLACK, JOHN. Banff, 1827-79, and sometime at Turriff, ABD. Wpr.- J. BLACK / WATCH MAKER / AND / JEWELLER / BANFF. Orn. bdr.

BLACK, JOHN. Auchinblae, KCD, ca. 1850 - ca. 1890. Wpr.- JOHN BLACK / PRACTICAL / WATCHMAKER / & JEWELLER / AUCHINBLAE. Str. & bkl. bdr., with advert for repairs. On the back, "1891: 2/6d".

BLACKADDER, J. WM & J, 21 New Market Gallery, 1895.

BLACKWOOD, A. WM & J, 52 Broad Street, Aberdeen, 1880-86. Poss. the craftsman later at 14 New Entry, Dundee.

BONNAR, JAMES. CM in Aberdeen, ca. 1780- ca. 1810. Sometime ptn. of GEORGE MORRISON. He m. Janet Ferguson. Daughter Catherine, bapt. by an Episcopalian clergyman, 1.1.1786.

BOOTH, GEORGE. CM, WM & J, Aberdeen, 1815. At 36 Union Street before 1830, when the firm became GEORGE BOOTH & SON. The son was prob. Alexander. There was also a son Joseph, 1803-71, who graduated at Marischal College in 1817, and became a WS. There may have been a son George. The craftsman resided at Springbank, Dee Street. He was a private in the Gilcomston Pikemen, 1803-08, and Deacon of the Inc. of Hmm., 1815-16.

BOOTH, GEORGE & SON. CM, WM & J, 38 Union Street, Aberdeen, 1830-40, and contd. until 1852, when WILLIAM BRANDS succ. to the business.

BOOTH, JAMES. C & WM, Auchinblae, KCD, 1837-61. He was a native of Banff and "the tallest man ever seen in any countryside". James m. Margaret Stephen, and d. testate, 2.2.1861. A daughter Mary resided at Fordoun.

BOOTH, JOHN. At 41 Kirkgate, Aberdeen, 1820-52, and at Black's Buildings in 1851, when he had two apprs. Wpr. - JOHN BOOTH / WATCH & CLOCK / MAKER / ABERDEEN. By his wife Elizabeth he had at least two children: 1. John, b. ca. 1835; 2. Jane, b. ca. 1844.

BOYD, A.W. Buckie, BAN, 1860-70. Wpr.- A.W. BOYD / WATCH MAKER / & JEWELLER / EAST CHURCH STREET / BUCKIE. Str. & bkl. Bdr., advertising repairs.

BRANDER, JAMES. C & WM, Keith, BAN, 1825-35. He was s/o George B., a merchant in Keith, and d. 11.3.1835, aged 47 years.

BRANDS, WILLIAM. J, SS & W-repairer, Aberdeen, 1852-64. Worked for GEORGE BOOTH & SON, 1831-51, and succ. to that business at 48 Broad Street. At 15 Huxter Row, 1861-64, when he ret. He resided at Chapel Lane, 1835, and at Carmelite Street, 1841-47. Sometime at Charlotte Street and latterly at Huxter Row. William was s/o Andrew B. and Elizabeth Primrose. He d. 8.7. 1866, and was bur. at St. Peter's Chyd., Spittal, Old Aberdeen.

BREMNER, WILLIAM. Kemnay, ABD, ca. 1885. Wpr.- Wm. BREMNER / WATCHMAKER / JEWELLER & OPTICIAN / KEMNAY. Str. & bkl. bdr., advertising repairs.

BROWN, JOHN. C & WM, Woodside, Aberdeen, prob. before 1826.

BRYDEN, THOMAS. C & WM, Johnshaven, KCD, 1837.

BUDGE, DANIEL. WM & J, Church Street, Portsoy, BAN, 1877.

BUDGE, JAMES. Keith, BAN, ca. 1880. Wpr.- JAMES BUDGE / WATCH / MAKER / & JEWELLER / 170 MID STREET / KEITH. Str. & bkl. bdr., advertising repairs.

BUGLAS, JAMES. C & WM, Keith, BAN, ca. 1885.

BURNETT, JOHN. CM & astronomer, Keithfield, Tarves, ABD, 1830-70. He was s/o Thomas B., cartwright, and Rachel Chapman. John m. Agnes Shepherd, 1820-57, with issue: 1. Rev. John, BD, b. 1844, minister of the Free Church of Premnay and Leslie, 1869-78, afterwards at St. David's, Glasgow; 2. Alexander, tea-planter in Ceylon. John d. at Gaudie Cottage, Premnay, 26.6.1891, aged 89 years.

BURNETT, W. C & WM, Aberchirder, BAN, ca. 1830. Poss. sometime at New Byth, ABD.

BURNETT, WILLIAM. C & WM, Fraserburgh, ABD, 1846.

C

CAIRD, DAVID. Auchinblae, KCD, 1840-53. Said to have learned his trade in Edinburgh, and to have made or finished a number of railway station clocks on the Edinburgh-Aberdeen line. He was b. 1819, and emigrated to America in 1853.

CALDER, MALCOLM. Appr. to George M. Carnaby, WM & J, Thurso, CAI, and became a jour. with PAUL WONDERLY, Aberdeen. Commenced business at 55a St. Nicholas Street, Aberdeen, 1879, as M. & S. Calder. The ptn. was his brother Sinclair. They were s/o James Traill C., crofter, and Jessie Gunn. Malcolm m. Margaret, d/o William Honeyman Henderson, blacksmith, and had issue: 1. James Sinclair, 1878-99; 2. William, WM with the family firm, but emigrated to New York; 3-4. Malcolm and Elizabeth Davidson, twins; 5. Janet; 6. Margaret, teacher. Malcolm was an elder and office-bearer of Bon Accord UF Church, and an active freemason. He d. at 61 Bonnymuir Road on 19.10.1908, aged 65 years.

CALDER, SINCLAIR. Ptn. with his brother MALCOLM C. He m. Bethia, d/o Ebenezer Bain, house carpenter, and emigrated to America, prob. New York.

CAMERON, HUGH. CM in Johnshaven, KCD, 1780-90. Clocks signed "Hugh Cameron, Johns Haven".

CAMPBELL, JOHN. C & WM, Kintore, ABD, 1860-80.

CARNEGIE, JAMES. Kinneff, KCD, 1838. Wpr.- CHEAP CLOCKS BY JAMES CARNEGIE, KINNEFF. Bro/o ROBERT C.

CARNEGIE, ROBERT. C & WM, Drumlithie, KCD, 1838. Bro/o the above.

CARNEGIE, ROBERT. C & WM, Auchinblae, KCD, 1803-37. Made clocks of superior workmanship, much prized in the district. He was a private in the Mearns Volunteers, 1803-08. He m. Margaret Wilkie, with issue.

CARNIE, ALEXANDER. WM & J, 29 Adelphi Street, Aberdeen, 1900+.

CARPENTER, J. WM & J, Aberdeen, 1900+.

CARR, J. WM & J, 7 Little Belmont Street, Aberdeen, 1900+.

CAVIN, ARTHUR. WM, J & OP, Fraserburgh, ABD, ca. 1885.

CENTER, WILLIAM. CM, Banchory-Ternan, ca. 1840.

CHALMERS, ALEXANDER THOMSON. C & WM, Aberdeen, 1836.

CHISHOLM, A.F. WM & J, 6 Correction Wynd, Aberdeen, 1877-87.

CHISHOLM, WILLIAM. Appr. in Aberdeen adm. to the Inc. of Hmm. there as CM, 13.10.1800. Adm. trade-B, 22.2.1801.

CLARK, GEORGE. C & WM, Aberdeen, d. 1852, aged 30 years.

CLARK, JOHN & SON. Laurencekirk, KCD, Late Victorian period. Wpr.- JOHN CLARK & SON / WATCHMAKERS / AND JEWELLERS / LAURENCEKIRK. Bdr. trimmed to fit small watch. On the back: "13.8.09". The son was Alexander C.

CLARK, WILLIAM. C & WM, Invergelder, Crathie, ABD, ca. 1800- ca. 1830. Bro/o Andrew C., farmer.

CLARK, WILLIAM GILLAN. Commenced business at 115 George Street, Aberdeen, 1875. At No.117 by 1877, and at No.65 in 1880. By 1883 at No.70, and at No.82, 1891-95. Afterwards at 1 Skene Place. Wpr.- W.G. CLARK / PRACTICAL / WATCHMAKER / JEWELLER &c. /115 GEORGE STREET / ABERDEEN. Fml. bdr. He m. Euphemia Watt, 1845-1900, and had issue. William d. 25.2.1910, aged 66 years.

CLERK, JAMES. Appr. to CHARLES LUNAN, C & WK, Aberdeen, for 9 years from 1.1.1799. There was no fee, and his cautioners were Thomas Gordon, mason, and James Thain, wright. He was s/o Gilbert C., then in Jamaica, and Isabel Gauld, who consented to the indentures.

COCKBURN, WILLIAM. Keith, BAN, ca. 1885. Wpr.- WILLIAM COCKBURN / WATCH- MAKER / AND / JEWELLER / MID STREET / KEITH. Str. & bkl. bdr., with advert for repairs.

COLLISON, WILLIAM. WM & J, Stonehaven, KCD, 1834-47.

CONWAY, S.F. WM & J, 63 Union Street, Aberdeen, 1897-1900+.

COOK, ALEXANDER. Dufftown, BAN, Mid Victorian period. Wpr. - [Square and compass] / ALEXANDER COOK / WATCHMAKER, JEWELLER AND OPTICIAN /10 COWAL STREET / DUFFTOWN. Double str. & bkl. bdr., inner advertising repairs. On the back: "3.9.64".

COOK, JAMES. C & WM, Strichen, ABD, 1846. Prob. related to George C., shoemaker there, 1845-65.

COOK, WILLIAM. With WILLIAM VANHAGEN, appointed to rule the town and kirk clocks of Aberdeen, 1651.

CORBET, JOHN. New DEER, ABD, ca. 1865-1900+. Wpr.- JOHN CORBET / WATCH / AND / CLOCK MAKER / NEW DEER. Orn. bdr. A later wpr. describes him as WM & J.

CORKEN, ARCHIBALD. C & WM, Cotton, Aberdeen, 1837.

CORKEN, WILLIAM. C & WK, 47 Hadden Street, Aberdeen, 1843-44. Prob. related to the above ARCHIBALD C.

COURAGE, ALEXANDER. Said to have been of Huguenot ancestry. Adm. freeman SS of the Inc. of Hmm. of Aberdeen, 11.6.1804, and as trade-B the same year.

COURAGE, JOHN. Appr. to PETER GILL, C & WM, Aberdeen, before 1815. Adm. a trade-B of Aberdeen, 1834. He was b. 1799, s/o Archibald C., wright, and his wife Isobel, and related to Alexander C., above. John worked in London for a time, but returned to Scotland to manage a business in Inverurie for a widow. He commenced business at Insch, and eventually owned property in that place, noted in a valuation roll of 1838. John m. Elspet, daughter of William Robertson, feuar in Insch, and Elspet Dalzell. She d. 28.2.1884, and John d.19.3.1858.

COUTTS, ALEXANDER MACKIE. Jour. WK in Aberdeen, 1900+. He was s/o JAMES C. and Bridget Mackie, and d. at Aberdeen Royal Infirmary, 20.11.1911, aged 35 years.

COUTTS, ANDREW W. WM & J, Aberdeen, 1890-1900+.

COUTTS, GEORGE. Kinord Loch, nr. Ballater, Deeside, ABD. A well-known local historian, he erected a water-clock at his home for the benefit of passer-by. It was driven by drops of water falling upon a copper bucket wheel, and kept good time. He m. Isabella Forbes, with issue, and d. 9.1. 1921, aged 69 years.

COUTTS, JAMES. WM & J, Aberdeen, 1874-1900+. Joined his brother JOHN C., at 34 Schoolhill, 1874. JOHN d. in 1879, and he traded as J. Coutts & Co., until ca. 1890, mainly at 6 Skene Street. He appears under his own name at 46 Holborn Street, during that year, and to after 1900. James resided at 69 Union Grove. He was b. ca. 1845, s/o Joseph C., mason, and Ann Callum. James m. Bridget Mackie, and d. 23.8.1903. Son ALEXANDER MACKIE C.

COUTTS, JOHN. CM, WM & J, Schoolhill, Aberdeen, 1858. After a period at Bridge Street, he was again at Schoolhill, No.34, in 1874, along with his brother JAMES C., trading as John & James C. until 1890. He d. unm. at 27 Charles Street, 17.11.1879, aged 52 years.

COUTTS, J. & F. WM & J, 29 St. Nicholas Street, Aberdeen, 1892-96.

CRAIGHEAD, ANDREW. Inverurie, ABD, 1855-86. Made clocks for railway stations in association with JOHN HUNTER. Wpr.- A. CRAIGHEAD / WATCH / AND / CLOCK MAKER / INVERURIE, Orn. bdr. On the back: "Jan. 1884". He ret. to Bath, Somerset, and d. there in 1919.

CROMBIE, JOHN. C & WM, Peterhead, ABD, 1860.

CRONE, WILLIAM. C & WM, Jack's Brae, Aberdeen, 1828-39; at Upper Denburn, 1840-51.

CRONE, WILLIAM. WM & J, 6 St. Nicholas Street, Aberdeen, 1880-86.

CRUICKSHANK, ALEXANDER. C & WM, 11 Upper Kirkgate, Aberdeen, before 1895. He d. 17.11.1903, aged 60 years.

CRUKSHANKE, JOHNE. Aberdeen, 1453. The earliest known name in Scottish horology. The *Burgh Council Records* contain the following entry: 22nd May 1453: *The samyn day hes grauntit the said aldermen and consaile to Johne Crukshanke, the seruice of kepying the orlage for this year, and til hafe til his fee t[he] service of it XLs., and hes sworne the gret athe to do his diligent besynes to the keping of it.*

CUMMING, JOHN. C & WM, Banff, adm. to the Inc. of Hmm. there, 1800. He was struck off the roll in 1808 for arrears of his "quarterly pennies".

CUMMING, RICHARD. C & WM, Alford, ABD, 1828.

CUMMINGS, JOHN. C & WM, Banff, 1780-1808.

D

DALLAS, GEORGE. C & WM, Insch, ABD, ca. 1876.

DALZEIL or DALZIEL, JAMES. C & WM, Fraserburgh, ABD, 1823-44. He subscribed for a copy of James Fordyce's *Hymns and Sacred Poems* (Aberdeen, 1787). James was a member of Saltoun Lodge Society of Gardeners.

DALZEIL, JAMES. C & WM, 2 Frederick Street, Aberdeen, 1823-26. At Ratties Court, 26 Broad Street, 1827-32; 13 Marischal Street, 1833, and at 51 Queen Street, 1844.

DAVIDSON, ROBERT. Appr. to WILLIAM ALLAN, C & WM, Aberdeen, for 5 years from 14.8.1766: fee £8 Sterling and bed clothes. He was s/o Alexander D. in Mains of Clakriach.

DAVIDSON, WILLIAM. Turriff, ABD, ca. 1890-1900+. Wpr.- Wm. DAVIDSON / CERTIFIED AS A / WATCHMAKER BY / CITY AND / GUILDS INSTITUTE / LONDON / CERTIFIED AS AN/ OPTICIAN BY WORSHIPFUL / COMPANY OF SPECTACLE / MAKES / LONDON / 37 HIGH STREET, TURRIFF. Str. & bkl. bdr., advertising repairs.

DAWSON, JOHN A. Laurencekirk, KCD, ca. 1880-1900+. Wpr.- JOHN A. DAWSON / WATCHMAKER / AND JEWELLER / HIGH STREET / LAURENCEKIRK. Double bdr., inner with advert for repairs. On the back: "718-14/11/07".

DEAN, WILLIAM. WM in Aberdeen, 1819, prob. jour. He was bur. at St.. Peter's Chyd., Spittal, 13.7.1819, aged 25 years.

DEMPSTER, ANDREW. Maud, ABD, ca. 1845-75. Wpr.- AND". DEMPSTER / WATCH MAKER / JEWELLER / & OPTICIAN, MAUD. Double bdr., inner str. & bkl., advertising repairs.

DEVERLEY, HUGH. C & WM, 7 Upperkirkgate, Aberdeen, 1850-56. Previously in Perth from ca. 1843.

DON, JOHN. C & WM, Turriff, ABD, Early Regency period.

DONALD, JAMES. Aberchirder, BAN, Late Victorian period. Wpr.- JAMES DONALD / WATCH / AND CLOCK MAKER / ABERCHIRDER. Str, & bkl. bdr., advertising repairs to musical boxes, jewellery, watches and clocks. On the back; "2244-30 Nov. 80".

DONALD, WILLIAM. Appr. to GEORGE SMITH, C & WK, Huntly, ABD, and may have worked as a jour. in Aberdeen, ca. 1832. Commenced business at Rhynie, in Huntly parish, and was making clocks until ca. 1870. He was b. 1807, s/o William D. and Helen Nicol. William m. (i) Isabel Hill, who d. 22.2.1837, aged 27 years, having had issue: 1. WILLIAM, Jr. ; 2. Jane, d. inf. He m. (ii) Elizabeth Kilgour, with further issue; 3. George; 4. Benjamin; 5. Mary; 6. Eliza; 7. Johnathan. William d. 11.9.1878, and was bur. in the Chyd. at Rhynie.

DONALD, WILLIAM. Jr. C & WM, ca. 1870. He was s/o the above William D., by his first wife. James worked for a time as a jour. in London, but returned to Rhynie, where he was also a photographer.

DUCAT, T. WM & J, 437 Gt. Western Road, Aberdeen, 1898-1900+.

DUFF, ALEXANDER. C & WM, 35 Upperkirkgate, Aberdeen, 1877.

DUFF, GEORGE. At 69 Nethergate, Aberdeen, before 1895, and at 17 St. Nicholas Street, 1895-1900+. Wpr.- GEORGE DUFF / WATCHMAKER / JEWELLER & CUTLER / 69 NETHERGATE / ABERDEEN. Orn. bdr.

DUFF, GEORGE. Stonehaven, KCD, ca. 1890. Wpr. – GEORGE DUFF / WATCHMAKER / & JEWELLER / STONEHAVEN. Str. & bkl. bdr., advertising repairs.

DUFF, JOHN. WM, adm. to the Inc. of Hmm. of Banff, 1811.

DUFFUS, BENJAMIN. CK, WM & J, 55-56 Market Gallery, Aberdeen, 1877-85, also at Upperkirkgate, 1886. At the latter address only in 1895, and by 1900 at 10 Back Wynd.

DUNCAN, ALEXANDER G. Aberdeen, ca. 1890-1900+. Wpr.- A.G. DUNCAN / WATCH- MAKER & / JEWELLER / 256 George Street / ABERDEEN. Triple bdr., outer stating certificated first class by City and Guilds, London Institute, in watch and clock making. Advert for repairs on inner bdr.

DUNCAN, ANDREW. CM in Aberdeen before 21.2.1824, when served heir general to his father, Andrew D., square-wright in Huntly.

DUNCAN, GEORGE. C & WM, 25 Bridge Street, Banff. He was adm. to the Inc. of Hmm. there, in 1816. In arrears with his dues, 1818, 1823 and 1832. He m. Ann Duncan, who d. 21.12.1827, aged 27 years. Chrn. incl.: 1. Ann, b. ca. 1818; 2. Mary, b. ca. 1820.

DUNCAN, JAMES. C & WM, Old Meldrum, ABD, 1781-95. Perhaps previously at Inverurie, where adm. B, 7.5.1761. Made a town clock for Stonehaven.

DUNCAN, JAMES. C & WM, Aberdeen, ca. 1800. Poss. related to JOHN D Turriff. He m. Isabella Black. Their daughter Helen, 1789-1858, m. JAMES MITCHELL.

DUNCAN, JOHN. C & WM, Turriff, ADB, ca. 1790-1830. Poss. related to JAMES D., Old Meldrum. John m. 17.9.1805, Nancy, d/o Peter Duff, HEICS, who brought with her a tocher of £900. She also received £600 by the will of John Duff of Crovie. John and Nancy had one child, Wilhelmina, who m. John Webster. Her portrait was painted by Andrew Robertson, 1777-1845.

DUNCAN, JOHN. C & WM, 25 Evan Street, Stonehaven, KCD, 1877.

DUNCAN, WILLIAM. WM & J, Rhynie, ABD, 1877.

DUNLOP, ANDREW. CM in Aberdeen, 1700. Went to London, and there until 1732.

DUNNINGHAM, WILLIAM. CM, WM & J, Aberdeen. He was a ptn. of SANGSTER & DUNNINGHAM, 78 Union Street, 1880, previously SANGSTER, SMITH & Co. By 1886, appears in the local directories as William D. & Co., same address. He moved to 35a Union Street by 1895, and at 33 Belmont Street, 1900+.

E

EASTON, ALEXANDER R. CM, WM, NIM & OP, 53 Marischal Street, Aberdeen, ca. 1860-65, in succ. to JOHN McKILLICAN. At 9 Regency Quay, 1866-73.

EASTON, R. C & WM, Aberdeen, 1860.

EDELSHAIN, -----. C & WM, Aberdeen, 1885-1900+. Ptn., ZANEC & EDELSHAIN.

EDWARD, ROBERT. C & WM, Stonehaven, KCD, 1860.

ELDER, GEORGE. WM & J, 59 St. Nicholas Street, Aberdeen, 1880.

ELLEIS, DAVID. CM, Aberdeen, 1560.

EMSLIE, JAMES S. WM & J, 70 Schoolhill, Aberdeen, 1893-1900+.

EMSLIE, WILLIAM. WM & J, 124 George Street, Aberdeen, 1895-1900+.

ESSON, PETER. C & WM, Aberdeen, 1855-72. He tenanted a shop formerly occupied by HAY MERCER, and traded, 1858-62, at 27 West North Street. He was at No.7, 1863-71, and moved to No.4 shortly before he d., 3.8.1872. His son Peter, Jr., and daughter Helen, were served heirs general to him in a plot of land of Humphrey's Croft, on the west side of the town, 17.10.1872. They resided in Canal Street.

F

FALCONER, WILLIAM. C & WM, and W-materials manf., Laurencekirk, KCD, 1874.

FARQUHAR, ANDREW. C & WM, Marischal Street, Peterhead, ABD, 1837.

FARQUHAR, WILLIAM. WM & J, adm. to the Inc. of Hmm. of Aberdeen, 3.3.1837, and adm. trade-B, 10.3.1837. He was s/o John F., weaver-B.

FASKEN, ALEXANDER. WM & J, 17 New Market Gallery, Aberdeen, 1893-1900+.

FERGUSON, JAMES. C & WM, astronomer and author. This remarkable man was b. nr. Rothiemay, BAN, on 25.4.1710. s/o John F., day labourer, and Elspeth Lobban. In 1732 he made a wooden clock and a watch with wooden wheels and a whalebone spring. He moved to Edinburgh in 1734 and trained as a artist, becoming a portrait painter. While in the capital he made an ingenious astronomical machine. He went to London, ca. 1760, where he did much to popularise astronomy by lecturing and writing. He was elected FRS, and the king conferred on him a pension of £50 per annum. A collection of his scientific papers and ephemera came into the possession of his biographer, Ebenezer Henderson, the Dunfermline clockmaker and historian, and through Richard Cameron, bookseller in Edinburgh, was sold to New York Public Library in 1899. James m. (contr. dated 28.4.1739), Isobel Wilson, who d. 3. 9.1773, aged 55. Chrn: 1. Agnes, 1746-92; 2. James, 1748-72; 3. Murdoch, 1752-1803, surgeon; 4. John, graduated MA at Marischal College, Aberdeen, 1776. James d. 10.11.1776, and was bur. in Marylebone Chyd.

FILLAN, -----. C & WM, ptn. of FILLAN & WATSON.

FILLAN & WATSON. C & WM, 82 Union Street, Aberdeen, 1849-50.

FINDLAY, A & J. C & WM, New Market Gallery, Aberdeen, 1855.

FINDLAY, JOHN. WM & gem-dealer, 60 Queen Street, Aberdeen, 1832-36. At 30 Broad Street, as WM & manf. of silver plate, 1836-45. At New Market Gallery, 1845-50, also at 1 Queen Street. By 1855 became A. & J. FINDLAY. John was b. ca. 1802, and by his wife Margaret had issue: 1. Alexander, WM, b. ca. 1829; 2. John, b. ca. 1831, poss. in business with his brother Alexander, 1855; 3. Ann, b. ca. 1835; 4. Margaret, b. ca. 1837; 5. Charles, b. ca. 1840; 6. Mary, b. ca. 1843; 7. William, b. ca. 1846.

FINDLAY, JOHN. C & WM, Banchory-Ternan, ABD, ca. 1860.

FINNIE, WILLIAM L. WM & J, 20 Broad Street, Aberdeen, ca. 1882; at No. 24a, 1900+.

FIRTH, JOSEPH. CM, WM & J, 20 St. Nicholas Street, Aberdeen, 1880. Became Joseph F. & Sons.

FORBES, THOMAS. Strichen, ABD, ca. 1880. Wpr.- THOMAS FORBES / WATCH MAKER / & JEWELLER / HIGH STREET / STRICHEN. Str. & bkl. bdr., advertising repairs.

FORBES, WILLIAM. C & WM, Kintore, ABD, 1837-58. Alumnus, King's College, Aberdeen, 1808. He was s/o Theodore F., physician, and Margaret Shinney. William d. unm. in 1858.

FORSYTH, ANTHONY. WM & J, 210 King Street, Aberdeen, 1895.

FORSYTH, ROBERT. WM & J, 2 Belmont Street, Aberdeen, 1877.

FORSYTH, T.M. CM, Turriff, ABD, 1818-41; Aberdeen, 1842. He became an exciseman; later at London in the same service. He m. Jane Brands. Son William, 1818-97, poet, and sometime editor of *The Aberdeen Journal*.

FORSYTH, WILLIAM. C & WM adm. to the Inc. of Hmm. of Aberdeen, 1811. He was bur. in St. Peter's Chyd., Spittal, 29.7.1819, aged 38 years.

FOWLER, P.S. Asleed, Methlick, nr. Ellon, ABD, ca. 1890. Wpr.- P.S. FOWLER / WATCHMAKER / AND JEWELLER / ASLEED / BY METHLICK. Str. & bkl.

FRASER, ALEXANDER. Aberdeen, 1830-35. Wpr.- ALEXANDER FRASER / WATCHMAKER / AND / JEWELLER / 38 UPPERKIRKGATE / ABERDEEN. Plain double bdr., with advert for gold and silver scarf pins, brooches and rings.

FRASER, JOHN. 166 Union Street, Aberdeen, 1823-31; 1 Crown Street, 1832- 43; 166 Union Street, 1844-54; and at 170 Union Street, 1855-70. Wpr.- JOHN FRASER / WATCH & CLOCK / MAKER /170 UNION STREET / ABERDEEN. Orn. bdr. On the back: "Aug. 1868". He resided at Whitehouse Terrace until1860, afterwards at Balmoral Place. John m. Elizabeth Dawson and predeceased her. She d. at Walthamstow, Essex, 1.4.1892, aged 68 years.

FRASER, JOHN A. Dufftown, BAN, ca. 1890. Wpr.- Perpetual calendar in the centre, and on a plain bdr. JOHN A. FRASER / WATCHMAKER / JEWELLER / DUFFTOWN.

FRASER, ROBERT. WM in Aberdeen; sometime in Edinburgh. Bur. in St. Peter's Chyd., Spit tal, 20.8.1829, aged 33 years.

FREDERICK, CHARLES & BROTHERS. C & WM, 64 Broad Street, Aberdeen, 1850. Charles was a witness at the wedding of JOHN F. in 1846.

FREDERICK, JOHN & Co. German CMs, 38 Queen Street, Aberdeen, 1841-44; at Broad. Street, 1845-51. He was b. in Germany, ca. 1817, and was prob. related to CHARLES F. John m. 25.8.1846, Elizabeth, d/o the dec. James Mollison, shoemaker.

FREEMAN, CHARLES. Aberdeen, Late Regency and Earl Victorian periods. Wpr.- CHAs. FREEMAN / WATCH MAKER / & DEALER IN WATCHES / NORTH GALLERY / NEW MARKET / ABERDEEN. Fml. bdr. He m. Anastasia Power, who was bur. in St. Peter's Chyd., Spittal, 1849, aged 33 years.

FROST, WILLIAM. C & WM, Aberdeen, 1828.

FIFE, CHARLES. C & WM, Aberdeen, 1802.

G

GALL, THEODORE. C & WM, King Street, Aberdeen, 1844-46. No entry for him in the local directory for 1847, but a Mrs G. appears at 19 College Bounds, Old Aberdeen.

GALLOWAY, JOHN. CM in Aberdeen before 1725. His son Alexander m. (contr. dated 1.2.1729), Janet, d/o William Henderson, merchant in Aberdeen.

GAMMACK, JAMES. C & WM, Main Street, Aberchirder, BAN, 1846. He emigrated to Ontario, Canada, ca. 1848, and took a farm in Westminster Township. James, m. Ann, sist/o Alexander Smith in Turriff, to whom she was served heir general, 1.7.1879. They had issue: 1. Alexander; 2. Anne; 3. James; 4. Robert; 5. William. James d. 23.12.1859, aged 62 years.

GARDEN, JOHN. C & WM, 14 St. Nicholas Street, Aberdeen, 1825-30, and resided at No.12. At 72 Broad Street, 1831-42. He was adm. a freeman of the Inc. of Hmm. of Aberdeen, 1827, and as a trade-B, 21.10.1831. Appears as a Parliamentary voter, 1840-42. He was s/o George G., weaver-B.

GARDNER, -----. C & WM, Longside, ABD, ca. 1820.

GARTLY, JOHN. C & WM adm. to the Inc. of Hmm. of Aberdeen, 22.11.1783. Adm. trade-B, 17.8.1785. His business premises were at 7 Huxter Row, and he resided at Burnett's Court, 5 Exchequer Row. John was a celebrated maker of turret clocks, which included examples at Old Machar Cathedral (1799); Fraserburgh Town (1804); King's College, Old Aberdeen (1811), and Aberdeen Tolbooth (1817). He is credited with another at Blairs College. He was noted for making pinions and axles, and perfected a hardening process. Poor health contributed to financial embarrassment, and he became a superannuated member of the Inc. of Hmm. John m. Katherine Morrison, and d. 3.9.1827, leaving issue.

GAULD, HARRY. Schoolmaster and poet, b. at Castlehill, Auchindoir, in 1791, s/o Harry G. After learning watchmaking, he worked at his trade in Rhynie from 1820-30. In 1828 he published a volume of poems. About 1830 he m. Mary, d. 17.1.1871, d/o John Ross, a crofter, and moved to Lumsden. There he taught school, and was appointed sub-postmaster at £10 yearly. He d. at Lumsden, 11.12.1873, and was interred at Auchindoir Chyd.

GAULD, JAMES. Alford, ABD, Mid and Late Victorian periods. Wpr.- ca. 1890: JAMES GAULD / WATCH MAKER / & JEWELLER / ALFORD. Str. & bkl. bdr.

GEDDIE, JOHN. C & WM, Banff, 1806-16. Adm. to the Inc. of Hmm. there, 1806. May have previously been in Huntly. In financial difficulties during the depression following Waterloo, and emigrated to Pictou, Nova Scotia, Canada, 1816. He d. before 1846. His son, Rev. John G., 1815-72, was a missionary to the New Hebrides, and was bur. at Geelong, Australia.

GERRARD, WILLIAM. Appr. to JAMES DALZEIL, Fraserburgh, ABD, before 1810, and was in business in The Square, Turriff, ca. 1820-70. Wpr.- GERRARD / WATCH MAKER / TURRIFF. Fml. bdr. On the back: "Sept./46". He was s/o Arthur G., schoolmaster at Grange, BAN, and b. 19.3.1790. William owned his own shop and was an office-bearer in Trinity Free Church. His wife Ann predeceased him, and he d. 14.3.1879.

GERRARD, WILLIAM. C & WM in Banff, 1836.

GIBB, GEORGE. New Machar, ABD, ca. 1835. Wpr.- GEORGE GIBB / WATCH / AND CLOCK / MAKER / NEW MACHAR. Orn. bdr.

GIBSON, WILLIAM. C & WM, Aberdeen, ca. 1795.

GILL, ALEXANDER. CM, WM & J, 69 Union Street, Aberdeen, 1860-87; 12 Bridge Street, 1888-1900+. Wpr.- ALEXR. GILL / WATCH / AND CLOCKMAKER / 69 UNION STREET / *next Royal Hotel* / ABERDEEN. Orn. triple bdr., inner with advert for gold and silver chains, lockets, brooches and rings. On the back: "August 5th 1875".

GILL, DAVID. C & WM, Aberdeen, 1824-74. Commenced business with his father, PETER G., ca. 1824, and later became a Ws. dealer in clocks at 13 Queen Street. With ptn., JAMES SMITH, as Gill & Smith, 1850-61. Became David G. & Son, 17 Union Street, 1861. David purchased in 1857, the lands of Blair Ythan and Savock, in Foveran parish, from Major Andrew Robertson. He was a commissioner of supply for Aberdeenshire, and for nearly sixty years a magistrate. For some time he was an officer in the Aberdeenshire Militia. He m. 20.11.1838, Margaret, d/o Gilbert Mitchell in

Savock and Haddo, and had issue: 1. David, 1843-1914, a distinguished astronomer, who was knighted in 1900, and succ. to Blair Ythan, sold in 1920; 2. Peter; 3. Andrew J. Mitchell of Auchinroath, Rothes; 4. James Bruce, b. 1849. David d. 6.4.1878, aged 89, and was bur, beside his wife in Foveran Chyd.

GILL, PETER. Appr. to GILBERT BANNERMAN, C & WM in Banff, ca. 1768. He was s/o Peter or Patrick G. , mariner, Fraserburgh. Commenced business at Aberdeen in 1773, and was adm. to the Inc. of Hmm. there, 5.9.1783. He appears as a member of the Narrow Wynd Society in 1791. In 1824 his son DAVID joined him. They erected a tower clock at Banchory-Ternan in 1827. Peter was b. ca. 1756, and d. at Union Terrace, Aberdeen, 26.1.1850.

GILLAN, JOHN. C & WM, Keith-hall, Inverurie, ABD, before 1837. He was at High Street, Keith-hall, in 1846, and d. testate, 11.9.1847.

GILLANDERS, WILLIAM. C & WM, Hosefield, Aberdeen, 1832-40. He was s/o John G. and Janet Ogilvie. Son WILLIAM G., Jr.

GILLANDERS, WILLIAM, Jr. Adm. to the Inc. of Hmm. of Aberedeen, 18.1.1834, and commenced business at 78 Union Street. At Eastfield, 1835-37, and at Hosefield, 1837-49.

GILLET, HUGH. Appr. to GEORGE ROBERTSON, CM in Aberedeen, for 6 years from 1.6.1783, for a fee of L.100 Scots, and to keep himself in wearing apparel. He seems to have thought himself of French ancestry, and signed a known clock "Heu Guillemot". He was s/o James G., a schoolmaster in Aberdeen.

GOODLAD, J.A. WM & J, 12a Correction Wynd, Aberdeen, 1898-1900+.

GORDON, ADAM. CM in Aberdeen, 1594-95, and 1600-1602 with ptn. DAVID ROBERTSON.

GORDON, ALEXANDER. Fife-Keith, BAN, Early and Mid Victorian periods. Poss. sometime in Duff town. Wpr.- A. GORDON / WATCH / AND / CLOCK MAKER / FIFE- KEITH. Orn. bdr. On the back: "24th Feb.1854".

GORDON, ALEXANDER. WM & J , Insch , ABD, 1877.

GORDON, ALEXANDER. WM & J, MacDuff, BAN, 1890-1900+. He was a nephew of PETER G., Huntly. His daughter Eliza d. at 127 Gellymill Street, MacDuff, 16.9.1921, aged 21.

GORDON, HUGH. CM in Aberdeen, 1748-90. Worked in London and Edinburgh before commencing business at Broadgate, 1748. Made many public and church clocks, incl. one for St. Nicholas Church, Aberdeen, at a cost of £120. He m. (contr. dated 21.12.1758), Margaret, d/o George Leslie of Rothie. Hugh d. 1.1.1790, and was bur. in St. Nicholas Chyd.

GORDON, HUGH. C & WM, Aberdeen, 1770-90. Prob. the man who was Deacon of the Inc. of Hmm., 1777. He m. in 1775, Clementine Smith, and had a daughter Jane, who m. John Craig of Mugiemoss, Sheriff Clerk of Aberdeen. Hugh owned the estate of Drimmies, which he disponed to his son-in-law in 1786.

GORDON, HUGH. Appr. to PETER GILL, CM in Aberdeen, ca. 1780, perhaps informally. After serving his appr. he joined the HEICS, returning to Aberdeen in 1803. He does not appear to have practised his trade. Hugh was b. 1766, s/o James G., Old Meldrum, and Jean Gordon. He purchased the lands of Woodhall, Inverurie, in 1808, re-naming the estate Manar. Hugh m. 2.4. 1807, Elizabeth, d/o Dr Thomas Arbuthnott, and had issue as detailed in J.M. Bulloch's *House of Hordon*, vol. 1. He d. at Manar, 11.7.1834.

GORDON, JAMES. C & WM, Gallowgate, Aberdeen, 1820. Poss. the craftsman adm. to the Inc. of Hmm., 2.3.1819. He went to Commers, Midmar, and d. before 7.5.1869, leaving his estate to his son James, Jr., with the residue to charities, mainly connected to the Free Church of Scotland.

GORDON, JOHN. Appr. to his uncle, PETER GORDON, C & WM, Huntly, ca. 1862, and commenced business in Old Meldrum. Chrn. incl. Donald, 1901-69, Governor, Bank of Canada, and President, Canadian National Railways.

GORDON, JOHN. WM & J, 161 George Street, Aberdeen, 1880.

GORDON, PETER. Appr. to his uncle, WILLIAM G., C & WK, Huntly, ABD. He was sometime a jour. with Robertson of Kingsland Road, London, and took up his trade in Huntly, 1880-92, but went again to London. He had served for three years on the Polic Commission, and in the Volunteers, before joining the London Scottish. Wpr.- Drawing of the ruins of Balvenie Castle, Dufftown, with the motto FVRTH FORTVIN AND FILL THE FATRIS. On a tablestone below, PETER GORDON / WATCHMAKER / DUFFTOWN. Fml. bdr. Another has a drawing of the new mansion of Balvenie, afterwards part of a distillery. The drawings were executed by his uncle, WILLIAM G. Peter was s/o John G in Dufftown, and Isabella Garrow. A daughter, Mrs Isabella Curtis, edited a newspaper in Washington, DC, USA.

GORDON, THEODORE. Appr. C & WM in Aberdeen, ca. 1805, after which he went to London, where he made horozontal and duplex escapements. He was sometime editor of *The Horological Magazine.* Theodore was a natural s/o Theodore G., Inspector of Army Hospitals, and lived 1789-1870. He was a beneficiary of the will of his aunt, Miss Jane G., of Ythan Lodge, Foveran, confirmed 19.3.1835.

GORDON, THOMAS. CM in Aberdeen, Late Georgian period. He subscribed for a copy of *Hymns and Sacred Poems,* by James Fordyce, published in 1787.

GORDON, WILLIAM. CM, WM & EG, Convel Street, Dufftown, BAN, 1825. He and WILLIAM ROSS were for a time jour. with JOHN GARTLY, in Aberdeen, and he was associated with WILLIAM MARSHALL in the making of longcase clocks for Gordon Castle. Wpr.- Compass, square, and other ornaments between columns / Wm. GORDON / WATCHMAKER / DUFFTOWN. Orn. bdr. On the back: "Dec.1855". A later wpr. is very ornate, having a surround of nine panels, some containing ryme. An outer bdr. has drawings of agricultural implements, and he describes himself as a "copperplate printer". The wprs. were his own work, and he executed others for his nephew, PETER G. William was s/o John G., farmer, and Christian Cruickshank. He m. Susan Kiloh, who d. 6.7.1864, and d. testate, 23.2.1864, aged 76 years.

GORDON, WILLIAM. C & WM, Mortlach, BAN, 1847-48.

GORDON & DONALD. Ws WM & J, 14 St. Nicholas Street, Aberdeen, 1895-1900+.

GORDONE, THOMAS. CR & gunsmith, Aberdeen, 1595.

GRANT, ALEXANDER. GLS & J, Aberdeen, 1825, and prob. sold watches. He lived 1802-54, and m. Ann Gordon, 1803-37, with issue.

GRANT, JAMES. Cullen, BAN, 1865-80. Wpr.- JAMES GRANT / WATCH MAKER / REIDHAVEN St. / CULLEN. Str. & bkl. bdr., advertising repairs.

GRANT, JAMES. C & WM, Fraserburgh, ABD, 1869.

GRANT, JOHN. Fyvie, ABD, 1846-48. Sometime at Gardenston, BAN, and perhaps briefly at Leith, MLN. At Fraserburgh, ABD, 1853-59, and at Broad Street, Aberdeen, 1860-80. Wpr.- JOHN GRANT / WATCH AND CLOCK / MAKER / FRASERBURGH. Double str. & bkl, bdr., inner with advert for compasses and wedding rings. John was s/o John G., farmer, and Elspeth Horne. He m. Ann Caroll, with issue, and d. at Broad Street, Aberdeen, 24.5.1889, aged 74 years.

GRANT, JOHN. C & WM, Quay, Aberdeen, 1865.

GRANT, JOHN. Aberdeen, 1875-1900+. At 51, later at 25 Castle Street. Wpr.- JOHN GRANT / WATCH MAKER / AND / JEWELLER / 61 CASTLE STREET / ABERDEEN. Orn. bdr.

GRANT, ROBERT. DM, 24 Frederick Street, Aberdeen, 1831-48.

GRANT, WILLIAM. Hatton of Fintry, ABD, 1825-50. He was a native of Peter head, s/o Alexander G., farmer, and Ann Hay. William m. Janet Moir, and had issue: 1. John, dy; 2. William; 3. Elspet; 4. Ann; 5. Margaret, dy; 6. Jane, dy; 7. Christian; 8. Jane (ii), dy. William d. 18.1.1855, aged 75 years, and was bur. at Fintray.

GRANT, WILLIAM. Huntly, ABD, Late Victorian period. At Duke Street, 1881. Owned property in Gordon Street, let to Dr Garson, at £35 per year. Wpr.- Wm. GRANT / WATCHMAKER / AND JEWELLER / HUNTLY. Str. & bkl, bdr., with advert for repairs. On the back: "February, 1895". In a note to Andrew Macpherson, his 'man of business', Union Street, William states he was b. 2.12.1854.

GRAY, ALEXANDER. C & WM, Aberdeen, 1850-1900+. Matriculated at Marischal College, 1815. Served his appr. and became a jour. with John Barron; then as ptn., 1847-48. In business at 11 Nethergate, 1850-95, then moved to No.20. Wpr.- ALEXr. GRAY / *Late Barron & Gray* / WATCH / AND / CLOCK / MAKER / 20 NETHERGATE / ABERDEEN. Str. & bkl. bdr. advertising repairs. He witnessed baptisms of Donald chrn. in the Episcopal Church between 1846 and 1859.

GRAY, ANDREW. CM, Aberdeen, 1717-63. John Rickart, 1671-1741, at Auchnacart, merchant in Aberdeen, paid him 7s. Sterling, 20.10.1749, for "keeping my watch and clock".

GRAY, CHARLES W. Appr. to ALEXANDER SIMPSON, and was in business at Fraserburgh, 1870-1900+. Wpr.- On a shield with a floral surround: CHARLES W. GRAY / JEWELLER / WATCH & CLOCK / MAKER / FRASERBURGH. Plain bdr. advertising large stock of watches, clocks and jewellery.

GRAY, JAMES. CM, NIM & WM, 38 Shore Street, MacDuff, BAN. Served his appr. at Montrose, and became a jour. with ----- LEASK, at MacDuff. Succ. him in the business, 1825. Purchased property at Shore Street, and served on the Town Council for some years. Wpr.- JAMES GRAY / WATCH / AND / CLOCK / MAKER / MACDUFF. Fml. bdr. He d. 18.2.1874, aged 72 years. Son James contd. the business.

GRAY, JOHN. Portsoy, BAN, Early Victorian period. Wpr.- JOHN GRAY / WATCH & CLOCK *I* MAKER / PORTSOY. Figure of 'Brittania' on the dexter side, and on top a bracket clock with 'Father Time' above. On the back: "21 Sept. 52".

GRAY, WILLIAM. CM in Aberdeen, ca. 1720.

GRAY, WILLIAM. C & WM Huntly, ABD, 1770-99. He was s/o William G., farmer in Skellarts, Daviot parish, and Jean Duncan, and d. 1799.

GREEN, ALEXANDER. Aberdeen, 1882-1900+. At 165 George Street, 1885; and at No.239 by 1899. Resided at 4 Eden Place, and after 1891 at 8 Loanhead Place. Wpr.- On a shield: ALEXR. GREEN / WATCH MAKER / JEWELLER / AND OP TICIAN / 239 GEORGE STREET / ABERDEEN. Fml. Bdr., adverising repairs to clocks and watches. He was b. at Tough, ABD, in 1859, s/o William G., a saddler, and Margaret Berry. Alexander m. at Aberdeen, 10.1.1883, Maggie, aged 23, d/o James Laing, tailor, and Margaret Beverly. Son ALEXANDER WILLIAM.

GREEN, ALEXANDER WILLIAM. Son of ALEXANDER G. and Maggie Laing, and b. 13.4.1884. Succ. to his father's business at 239 George Street, Aberdeen. He m. Cecilia Taylor, with issue, and d. a widower at Ladybank, FIF, 18.12.1973.

GREENBURY, H.L. WM & J, 88 Union Street, Aberdeen, 1886.

GREIG, DAVID. Stonehaven, KCD, 1835-46. Wpr.- DAVID GREIG / WATCHMAKER / ANN STREET / STONEHAVEN. Fml. shaded bdr.

GREIG, FRANCIS JOSEPH. CM in Aberdeen, prob. jour., d. 29.4.1850, aged 27.

GREIG, J. WM & J, 38 Evan Street, Stonehaven, KCD, 1900+.

GREIG, WILLIAM. CM, WM and feuar, Stewartfield, Old Deer, ABD, 1830-70. He d. unm., 6.1.1874, leaving a sum of money to Aberdeen University to found a bursary of £10 annually to any person of his surname who could prove a relationship; any person of his surname who was of good moral character and ability who was a native of Old Deer; or to any young Scot. The bursary became operable in 1882.

GREY, ERNEST. Aberdeen, 1848, formerly of Calcutta, India. He partly constructed and superintended work on an astronomical clock destined for the Missionary Institution associated with Dr Duff's library at Calcutta.

H

HAMILTON, WILLIAM. Appointed to undertake work on the church clock of Old Aberdeen, 1705-6. Afterwards in Leith, MLN.

HARDIE, JAMES. C & WM, 121 Barron Street, Woodside, Aberdeen, 1842-43; at Hadden Street, 1844-54. Appointed Sub-Postmaster, 1849. Emigrated to Australia, ca. 1855, with his wife and a sister-in-law.

HARDY, GEORGE. Old Deer, ABD, Mid Regency period. Wpr.- GEO. HARDY / WATCH / AND CLOCK MAKER / OLD DEER. Fml. bdr., with plain band containing regulating instructions. On the back: "Oct.25 1821".

HARDY, GEORGE. CM, WN & SS, Fraserburgh, ABD. Inscribed a silver plate for the laying of the foundation stone of the south pier at Fraserburgh, 1818. His name appears on the dials of a number of 8-day clocks.

HARDY, JAMES. C & WM, 14 Union Street, Aberdeen, 1860; at No.41 in 1865, and moved to No.53 by 1880. Became James Hardy & Son before 1895.

HARDY, JOHN. C & WM, 17 Huxter Row, Aberdeen, 1827-39. Succ. JOHN GARTLY. He d. in 1839, and his widow contd. the business until their son WILLIAM H, took over the work.

HARDY, WILLIAM. C & WM, 17 Huxter Row, Aberdeen, 1853; at 27 West North Street, 1855. He was s/o JOHN H., and d. 30.1.1860, aged 32 years.

HARVEY, N.L. Aberdeen, 1873, and sometime at Cuminestown, MOR. Wpr.- On a scroll, N.L. HARVEY / PRACTICAL / WATCH MAKER / JEWELLER &c. / 46 HOLBURN STREET / ABERDEEN. Str. & bkl. bdr., advertising cleaning and repairing clocks and watches.

HAY, ALEXANDER. DM & japanner, Aberdeen, 1828-48. May have succ. to the business of WILLIAM HAMILTON. At 16 Carmelite Street, 1828, then at Upperkirkgate, 1831-37. Latterly at 8 Thornton Place, Guestrow. He did much work for M. RETTIE & SON.

HAY, GEORGE. Buckie, BAN, ca. 1863. Wpr.- Bracket clock with crowing cock on top / GEORGE HAY / WATCH & CLOCK / MAKER / BUCKIE. Fml. bdr.

HAY, PATRICK. WM at Stewartfield, Old Deer, ABD, 1830-60. He was s/o Patrick H., grocer, and Barbara Taylor, and d. unm. 1.10.1861, aged 71 years.

HAY, THOMAS. C & WM, Peterhead, ABD, ca. 1860-69. He was s/o James H., cabinet-maker, and Ann Shewan. Thomas m. Jane McDonald, and d. 10.10.1869, aged 37 years.

HEITZMAN, FELIX. C & WM, 10 George Street, Aberdeen, ca. 1846.

HENDERSON, WILLIAM. Strichen, ABD, ca. 1885-90. Wpr.- Wm. HENDERSON / WATCHMAKER / JEWELLER / AND / OPTICIAN / STRICHEN. Str. & bkl. bdr., with advert for repairs to watches and jewellery.

HENDRY, JAMES. C & WM, Keith, BAN, before 1833. Noted for his pedantry and called 'Little Henry'. He is said to have dropped the D in his name to imitate the portly King Henry VIII, and this spelling is reflected in his entry in John Smith's work. James owned property in Bridge Street. He is stated to have emigrated to America before 1860.

HENDRY, JAMES. Prob. served his appr. with DAVID SUTHERLAND, C & WM in Keith, BAN, before 1820, and commenced business there. He was s/o James H., carrier, and Jane Lobban. James, who is sometimes confused with the above JAMES HENDRY, was sometime an auctioneer. Wpr.- JAS. HENDRY / WATCH & CLOCK MAKER / KEITH. Fml. bdr. On the back: "31st May 1850". He was in business until ca. 1870. In 1830 he m. Mary Duncan. Known chrn: 1. Alexander; 2. James, Jr., 1833-70; 3. Margaret, 1834-1914; 4. William; 5. Jean[nie], 'the belle of Keith', who m. Robert Gordon, of Keith, who migrated to Galashiels in 1867, and became a ptn. in the firm of Keddie & Gordon, Rosebank Tweed Mill. 6. George, 1841-1901, auctioneer and Inspector of the Poor, Keith.

HEPBURN, JOHN M.H. New Deer, ABD, ca. 1860-85. Wpr.- JOHN M.H.HEPBURN / WATCH MAKER / JEWELLER / & OPTICIAN / NEW DEER. Orn. bdr., with strap and bkl. bdr. advertising rings and jewellery.

HERD, J. Keith, BAN, ca. 1870. Wpr. - J. HERD / WATCHMAKER / AND / JEWELLER / MID STREET / KEITH. Surround of foliage with escrolls lettered: SEALS * KEYS * CHAINS * GOLD RINGS. Outer bdr. advertising silver and silver-plated goods, barometers and cutlery.

HIRD, BENJAMIN. C & WM, Kincardine O'Neil, ABD, 1896-1900+.

HORN, ALEXANDER. C & WM, Fyvie, ABD, ca. 1825. A self-taught CM, who was s/o Alexander H. and Jane Pratt. He m. Jane Castle, with issue, and d. 1.1.1887, aged 69 years.

HUNTER, JOHN. Inverurie, ABD, ca. 1855. He made a number of clocks for railway stations, in association with ANDREW CRAIGHEAD, who carried on the work when John became an inn-keeper on Deeside.

HUTCHEON, ALEXANDER. At 3 Schoolhill, Aberdeen, 1895, afterwards at No.6. Wpr.- ALEXR. HUTCHEON / WATCHMAKER / JEWELLER / & OPTICIAN / 3 SCHOOLHILL / ABERDEEN / REPAIRS UNDER PERSONAL SUPERVISION. Orn. bdr.

HUTCHEON, JOHN. Appr. to WILLIAM WATSON, Sr., Fyvie, ABD, 1893. Jour. WM at Dunfermline, FIF, 1898, afterwards at Cowdenbeath. Commenced business at East Register Street, Edinburgh, 1910. Went to Fyvie, 1914, to take over the business of his father-in-law. John m. 1900, Mary, d/o William Watson, Sr. Son John, WM in Boston, MA, USA.

HUTCHEON, -----. C & WM, Arbuthnott, KCD, ca. 1820. Poss. sometime at Kinneff.

I

INGRAM, GEORGE. C & WM, Gamrie, BAN, ca. 1790-1815. Some of his clocks are signed 'George Ingram, Gerdenstown'. Son WILLIAM I.

INGRAM, JOHN. C & WM, was b. at Cairney, nr. Huntly, ABD, and prob. served his appr. in ABD. His brother, Alexander I., of Leith, author and mathematician, left him his library and a sum of money. He went to Abergavenny, Monmouth, Wales, in 1796, and was still in business in 1830. Son John, WM.

INGRAM, WILLIAM. C & WM, Gardenstown, Gamrie, BAN, 1828-43. He was s/o GEORGE I., and m. 2.1.1830, Barbara Andrew, of King Edward parish, who d. 21.2.1870. Chrn: 1. George, 1833-1912, fish-curer in Gardenstown, but a cooper in 1868, when served heir in special to his father, and heir general to him in a tenement in Gardenstown; 2. Barbara, d. 1866. William d. 12.6.1843, aged 43 years.

INNES, Mrs F. New Maud, ABD, Late Victorian period. Prob. widow of a craftsman. Wpr.- MRS F. INNES / WATCHMAKER / & JEWELLER / NEW MAUD. Plain bdr., with ryme. On the back: "21.10.90".

INNES, GEORGE. Appr. to GEORGE ANGUS, CM in Aberdeen, 1807, and adm. to the Inc. of Hmm. there, 26.9.1817. Trade-B, 12.9.1821. In business as CM, WM and astronomical calculator at Skene Street, 1821-41. Resided at 2 Skene Street, 1829-30, and at No.7, 1831-41. He was interested in scientific research, and compiled *Tide Tables*, 1821. George contributed to periodicals and was elected FRAS in 1837. His book, *Meteorological Observations for 1840*, was published at Aberdeen in 1841. He was s/o James I., farmer, Rubislaw, and b. 1789. George m. Barbara Andrew, who d. 4.6.1838, aged 52. Chrn: 1. Elizabeth, 1819-75, served heir general to her father, 2.12.1868; 2. John William, 1823-35; 3. George, 1827-43. George, Sr., d. 22.5.1842.

INNES, GEORGE. C & WM, New Pitsligo, ABD, 1877.

INNES, JAMES. Appr. to his uncle, JOHN GORDON INNES, and was in business at Auchnagatt, ABD, 1850-1900+. He was s/o George I., farmer, and Margaret Wallace. Son Charles George, WM.

INNES, JOHN. WM, Aulditch Cottage, Inveravon, BAN, 1877.

INNES, JOHN GORDON. C & WM, Greenbrae, Auchnagatt, ABD, ca. 1800-62. Said to have learned the trade because of lameness. He went to Aberdeen and worked there as a jour. John was s/o James I., farmer in Greenbrae, and Jane Cantley. He d. unm., 1.6.1877, and was bur. at New Deer.

INNES, WILLIAM. WM, New Pitsligo, ABD, 1880-1900+. He was related to JAMES I., Auchnagatt, and d. 1.2.1920, aged 68 years,

INVERARITY, J. Banff, ca. 1890. Wpr.- J. INVERARITY / WATCHMAKER / JEWELLER & OPTICIAN / 35 LOW STREET / BANFF. On panels in the bdr. :

LARGE * VARIETY * WATCHES * CLOCKS * JEWELLERY * REPAIRS * CAREFULLY * EXECUTED * ON * THE * PREMISES.

IRVINE, WILLIAM. Prob. jour. with a C & WM in Aberdeen, ca. 1820.

J

JACK, A. & J. WM & J, 170 George Street, Aberdeen, 1885-95.

JACK, JAMES. WM & J, 395 Gt. Northern Road, Aberdeen, 1895.

JAFFRAY, ALEXANDER. C & WM, New Pitsligo, ABD, ca. 1860.

JAMIESON, GEORGE. Aberdeen, 1855-70. Wpr.- GEO. JAMIESON / JEWELLER TO THE QUEEN / 107 UNION STREET, ABERDEEN. Oblong scrollwork bdr. Became GEORGE J. & SON.

JAMIESON, GEORGE & SON. WM & J, SS & OP, 107 UNION STREET, ABERDEEN, 1870- 1900+. App. jeweller to Queen Victoria, and clockmaker to the Prince of Wales.

JAMIESON, JAMES. C & WM, Old Meldrum, ABD, 1840-60. He d. 23.10. 1860.

JAMIESON, WILLIAM. CM, Mill of Auchenhove, Udny, ABD, 1863.

JAMIESON, V.C. Buckie, BAN, ca. 1845. Wpr.- W.C. JAMIESON / WATCH MAKER / AND JEWELLER / CLEANING AND REPAIRS PROMPTLY EXECUTED / BUCKIE. Str. & bkl. bdr., unlettered.

JOHNSTON, JAMES. C & WM, Portsoy, BAN, ca. 1825-46. He subscribed for a copy of Thomas Anderson's *Poems and Songs: Chiefly in the Scottish Dialect* (Aberdeen, 1844). He d. 24.3.1846.

JOHNSTON, JOHN. Peterhead, ABD, 1815-48. Wpr.- JNO. JOHNSTON / WATCH & CLOCK / MAKER / PETERHEAD. He was s/o Alexander J., wright, and Helen Cruickshank. John d. 1848. Daughter Helen, 1806-95.

JOSS, S. WM & J, 41 Woolmanhill, Aberdeen, 1897-1900+.

K

KAY, JOHN. Lorimer in Aberdeen, mended the three town clocks of the town, 1582, and agreed to supply a new clock for 200 merks.

KEITH, WILLIAM. Appr. to JAMES BONNAR, C & WM, Aberdeen, for 5 years from 29.3.1791. Went to Inverness and commenced business there, prob. after a period as a jour. in Aberdeen.

KELMAN, CHARLES. C & WM, Aberchirder, BAN, 1877. Prob. rel. to WILLIAM K.

KELMAN, WILLIAM. Aberchirder, BAN, Early and Mid Victorian periods. Wpr.- Wm. KELMAN / WATCH / AND / CLOCK MAKER / ABERCHIRDER. Orn. bdr. On the back: "May 1864". Another has "Augt.1866".

KEMP, DAVID. C & WM, 53 Marischal Street, Aberdeen, 1855.

KENNEDY, JOHN. C & WM, Aberdeen, 1696. The *Poll-Tax Records* for Aberdeen show John K., stock under 5000 merks, for himself, wife, Isobel his daughter, servants Margaret Gordon and Isobel Allan, 12 merks each yearly: poll of £4: 8s Scots. The daughter Isobel m. 17.3.1702, Robert Fraser mariner.

KIDDIE, BENJAMIN. C & WM, Rose Street, Peterhead, ABD, 1846.

KILGOUR, PATRICK. This notable CM appeared in Aberdeen before 1672, when he applied for freedom to exercise his trade. He had come at the invitation of some of the burghers, and offered to make the Burgh Council a handsome 8-day brass clock, with "ane pendulum of the best form"; apparently a long pendulum, with anchor escapement, at that time new in Scotland. The Council allowed him to work free of taxes and impositions, but it was not until 1.12.1686 that he was adm. B, and he was obliged "not to midle or work in tyme coming any work belonging to any of the trades of the said burghs or their incorporations, only that it shall be leesom to him to make or mid watches or bells". He had settled in Old Aberdeen, and clearly had other talents. Patrick was app. town treasurer of Old Aberdeen for three years from 4.11.1679. He was apparently re-appointed, and on 3.11.1683, was instructed to have a purple coat, with white lace, and matching breeches, made for the town drummer. Although hampered by the powers of the Inc. of Hmm. of Aberdeen, the Council there nevertheless entered into an agreement with him, 9.11.1683, regarding the clock of St. Nicholas Church. He undertook to "translate the said clock into ane pendulum work conforme to the newest fashions and inventions done at London". He was to maintain it during his lifetime for payment of 40 merks yearly, but he had to furnish oil for the clock, and three bells in the steeple on his own charges. Patrick m. (i) Margaret Oren, who was bur. at Old Machar, 9.2.1686. The *Poll-Tax Records* of 1696 show that Patrick m. (ii) Widow Hamilton. The particulars are: "Patrick Kilgoure, watchmaker, stock under 5000 marks, for himself and wife, John, Mary and Anna Hamilton, her children; servants Margaret Mill and lsobell Lamb, 14 merks yearly, poll £5: 19s: 4d Scots." Patrick also had a son Thomas, adm. B of Old Aberdeen, 11.6.1685. He was prob. the C & WM who settled in Inverness, ca. 1697. The date of Patrick's d. has not been discovered. John Smith, in *Old Scottish Clockmakers,* gives a craftsman of this name at Canongate, Edinburgh, in 1702. This was prob. assumed, as on 20.3.1702, Marjorie, d/o Patrick Kilgour, WM, m. there, 20. 3.1702, David Dick, apothecary.

KILGOUR, WILLIAM. CM and weaver of bedcovers and tablecloths, at Glithno, nr. Fetteresso, KCD. He made a number of 8-day clocks "from beginning to end". He d. 12.3.1837, aged 86 years, and was bur. at Cowie, where there is a memorial.

KING, ALEXANDER. Peterhead, ABD, 1826. Moved to Dundee before 1840. He was related to Charles K., a Peterhead merchant, and he m. Janet Gray, who d. 2.9.1851, aged 47 years. Alexander d. at Dundee, 26.6.1842, aged 40 years.

KING, BENJAMIN. C & WM, Rose Street, Peterhead, ABD, 1846-48.

KING, JOHN. C & instrument maker, Tanfield Aberdeen, 1784-1807. By his wife Jean he had chrn: 1. Peter, b. 21.1.1784, d. inf.; 2. Jean, b. 17.8. 1785; 3. Ann, b. 14.8.1787. John was bur. at St. Peter's Chyd., Spittal, 7.5.1807, aged 46 years. His widow survived until 27.3.1849, then aged 85 years.

KIRKWOOD, JOHN. CM at Tor-na-Dee, Peterculter, ABD, ca. 1790.

KNOWLES, JOHN. C & WM, Ballater, Deeside, ABD, 1864-1900+. He worked in London, Isle of Wight, Huntly, Kincardine O'Neil and Aboyne. John was an ensign in the Marquess of Huntly's Highlanders, and later as a Lieut. in the Ballater Volunteers. He subscribed for a copy of Lewis Smith's *Parish of Birse* (Aberdeen, 1865). John was s/o William K., head gardener at Lessendrum, Huntly. He m. in 1864, Ann, d/o John

McIntosh, Rhynie, and d. 21.12.1905, aged 74 years. He was succ. in business by his son John.

L

LAING, JAMES. C & WM, Mid Street, Keith, BAN, 1837.

LAW, FREDERICK. Tarves, ABD, ca. 1885. Wpr.- FRED LAW / WATCH MAKER / & JEWELLER / TARVES. Str. & bkl. bdr. with advert for repairs.

LAW, JAMES. C & WM, Aberdeen. He m. privately, 22.11.1712, Barbara, d/o Robert ('Slowie') Burnet, glazier in Aberdeen.

LAW, JAMES. C & WM, Aberdeen, 1782.

LAW, JAMES B. Aberchirder, BAN, ca. 1890. Wpr.- JAMES B. LAW / WATCHMAKER / JEWELLER / OPTICIAN, ABERCHIRDER. Orn. bdr., advertising watches, clocks, cutlery and jewellery.

LAWS, JOHN. Adm. to the Inc. of Hmm. in Aberdeen as a WM, 29.7.1770.

LEASK, -----. C & WM, MacDuff, BAN, d. before 1825. Succ. by JAMES GRAY.

LEDINGHAM, ADAM. C & WM, Premnay, ABD, 1860-77.

LEYS, ALEXANDER. Appr. to his cousin, DAVID L., Kincardine O'Neil, ABD, and in business there, 1869-80. At Portsoy, BAN, 1880-1900+. Wpr.- ALEXR. LEYS / WATCH MAKER / & JEWELLER / PORTSOY. Str. & bkl. Bdr., advertising repairs. He was b. nr. Banchory, 1849, s/o Montgomery L., a crofter, and Isabella Dunn. Alexander d. in 1920. Son David.

LEYS, DAVID. Kincardine O'Neil, ABD, 1860-69. Moved to Portsoy, BAN, and then to Banchory, 1880. Wpr.- DAVID LEYS / WATCH & CLOCK / MAKER / SQUARE / PORTSOY. Orn. Bdr., with scrolls lettered: WATCHES * CLOCKS, JEWELLERY * SOLD AND * REPAIRED. On the back, "December lst 1877". He sold the business to his cousin, ALEXANDER LEYS, before 1860, and emigrated to America. David was s/o Alexander L., crofter on the Blackhall estate, nr. Banchory, and was b. ca. 1837. He d. at the home of his daughter, Mrs A.S. Christie, of Butte, Montana, 1.8.1921.

LEYS, DAVID. Torphins, ABD, and later at Kincardine O'Neil, ABD. where he took over the business of his brother, ALEXANDER L., in 1880. Afterwards at Cullen, BAN. Wpr.- DAVID LEYS / WATCH MAKER / & JEWELLER / TORPHINS. Str. & bkl. bdr., advertising repairs. He was b. 1852, and was alive in 1921.

LILLIE, WILLIAM. C & WM, Fraserburgh, ABD, ca. 1790.

LISTER, JOHN. WM & J, 46 Netherkirkgate, Aberdeen, 1877.

LITHGOW, JOHN. C & WM, Spittal, Old Aberdeen, before 1825. He m. Catherine McGregor, who d. 26.4.1825.

LITTLEJOHN, WILSON. WM & J, Peterhead, ABD, 1846. At several other locations, but returned to Peterhead, 1870. Moved to Stirling, 1876, and succ. DAVID TURNBULL at a cost of just over £2,000. He opened a branch at Dunfermline, FIF, in 1877, taking as ptn. his nephew HARRY L., and advertising also as an OP. The firm was dissolved the same year, and left with the nephew. Wilson's own business at Stirling went into liquidation in 1879, and the stock sold. He had a son [? William], a jour. WM living in Dunfermline in 1878, who emigrated to New Zealand.

LOGAN, WILLIAM. C & WM, Ballater, Deeside, ABD, 1825-60. He was s/o William L. and Jane Fraser, and m. Christian Keith before 1825. Their daughter Jane m. in 1865, Hugh Rose of Cairney and Shiels, Belhelvie. William ret. in 1860, and d. 26.2.1869, aged 79 years.

LOVIE, JOHN. WM & J, 46 Upperkirkgate, Aberdeen, 1897-1900+.

LOW, JAMES S. Turriff, ABD, Late Victorian period. Wpr.- JAMES S. LOW / WATCH MAKER / JEWELLER & OPTICIAN / HIGH STREET / TURRIFF. Plain bdr. with notice that watches bought or taken in exchange. On the back: "7 May 1897".

LUMSDEN, JAMES. CM in Aberdeen, 1740-65. His widow, maiden surname Gray, was bur. 20.2.1769.

LUMSDEN, JOHN. CM, Aberdeen, 1738-51. He m. (i) Margaret Farquharson, who d. 1739; (ii) Contr. dated 25.10.1742, Elizabeth Strachan, who d. 1765. He had several chrn. bur. in St. Nicholas Chyd., 1733-39. John was bur. there 16.2.1751.

LUMSDEN, WILLIAM. C & WM, Alford, ABD, 1677.

LUNAN, CHARLES. Appr. to HUGH GORDON, C & WM, Aberdeen, for 7 years from 20.3.1766. Adm. to the Inc. of Hmm., 1.10.1771, and entered as trade-B, 9.9.1777. Deacon of the Inc., 1795. He built a turret clock at Inverurie in 1774. A chamber clock by him is preserved in the Royal Museum of Scotland. His longcase clocks are noted for accuracy. This craftsman was often referred to as Charles L., Sr., to distinguish him from a contempory C & WM of the same name. He was s/o William L. in Monymusk, and he m. Mary Smith, with issue: 1. WILLIAM; 2. Isobel, b. 16.11.1774; 3. Ann, b. 18.7.1778; 4. Sarah, b. 10.6.1778; 5. Charlotte, b. 11.11.1779; 6. Elspeth, b. 4.5.1781; 7.[? James]. Charles was bur. 17.1.1816.

LUNAN, CHARLES. C & WM, Aberdeen, 1773-1823. He m. Mary Thomson. Their gr.-chrn., Ann and Bremner Hewitt, were served heirs to them, 8.3.1855.

LUNAN, JAMES. C & WM, King Street, Aberdeen, 1816-23. He was s/o CHARLES L., prob. the one who m. Mary Smith. James was a tertian at Marischal College in 1802. He was adm. freeman of the Inc. of Hmm., 1816, and entered as trade-B, 26.10.1818.

LUNAN, WILLIAM. C & WM, 8 Castle Street, Aberdeen, 1824-27; 5 Thistle Street, 1828-31, and at No.12 to 1834. He was a maker of philosophical instruments, and a globe friction electrical machine bearing his name is preserved in the Royal Museum of Scotland. He served in the Aberdeen Light Infantry Volunteers, 1799. William was s/o CHARLES L. and Mary Smith.

LUNDIE, JOHN. C & WM, Cotton, Aberdeen; 1825-28; Woodside, 1829-32, where he was also sub-postmaster. He was s/o WILLIAM L. and Elizabeth Robertson.

LUNDIE, WILLIAM. C & WM, Aberdeen, 1774. Adm. to the Inc. of Hmm. there, 1825, and as a trade-B, 1829. Moved to Inverurie, where he was also sub-postmaster. He was b. at Aberdeen, 1743, and m. Elizabeth Robertson, who d. 12.4.1856, aged 78 years. William d. 29.12.1816.

LYNDSAY, ALEXANDER. This man, poss. a Red Friar, mended and secured the town clock of Aberdeen in 1537, for which he was paid 5 merks. He seems to have been the man who worked also on clocks at Kinghorn and Falkland Palace, FIF.

Mc, MAC

McBEATH or McBETH, ALEXANDER. C & WM, High Street, Fraserburgh, ABD, 1837- 46. He was bro/o Charles M., agent for the Town & Country Bank, Fraserburgh. Alexander d. 13.11. 1846.

McDONALD, A. WM & J, 65 Victoria Road, Aberdeen, 1898-1900+.

MACDONALD, JAMES M. Portsoy, BAN, ca. 1888. Wpr.- Jas. M. MACDONALD / WATCHMAKER / & JEWELLER / SEAFIELD STREET / PORTSOY. Double str. & bkl. bdr., with advert for repairs.

MACDONALD, JOHN. Huntly, ABD, 1890-1900+. Wpr.- JOHN MACDONALD / WATCH- MAKER / JEWELLER & OPTICIAN / 13 DUKE STREET / HUNTLY. Str. & bkl. bdr., advertising repairs to clocks and watches.

McDONALD, JOHN S. New Pitsligo, ABD, Late Victorian period. Wpr.- JOHN S. McDONALD / WATCHMAKER / & JEWELLER / NEW PITSLIGO. Orn. bdr., inner rim advertising watches, clocks, jewellery and spectacles.

McDONALD, WILLIAM. WM & J, Strichen, ABD, 1877.

McFARLANE, THOMAS. C & WM, Ballater, Deeside, ABD, ca. 1860.

McGILLIVRAY, JAMES. CM, blacksmith, veterinary surgeon and author of books on the latter subject. At Alford, ABD, ca. 1840. Moved to Huntly, and later to Rayne. He was b. at Huntly, and lived 1800-80. He retired to Glasgow in 1875, with his son, William, a sculptor, sometime at Inverurie, father of the more famous sculptor, James Pittendrigh M., 1856-1938.

McGREGOR. A. Cullen, BAN, ca. 1865. Wpr.- A. McGREGOR / WATCHMAKER / JEWELLER & / OPTICIAN / 5 SEAFIELD STREET / CULLEN. Double fml. bdr., inner str. & bkl., with advert for watches, clocks and repairs.

MAC(K)INTOSH, GEORGE. Heckler at Woodside, Aberdeen, ca. 1860. He made a wooden clock, which kept good time. George was b.ca. 1834, s/o Francis M., a labourer of Highland extraction.

MACKAY, ALEXANDER. C & WM, Peterhead, ABD, 1798-1807. His brother John, farmer in Coynach, was served heir general to him, 7.2.1807.

McKAY, ALEXANDER. C & WM, Banff, 1771-81. Adm. to the Inc. of Hmm. there, 1775. He m. (contr. 3.12.1774), Lilia Morrison. Daughter Margaret d. 1775.

MACKAY, ALEXANDER SPENCE. OP in Aberdeen, became a ptn. of JAMES BERRY, 1879, and contd. at Marischal Street as sole owner after Berry d. in 1890. He lived 1857-1914. He was a gr.-son of JAMES T. MACKAY.

McKAY, ANDREW. C & WM, Fraserburgh, ABD, 1860.

MACKAY, JAMES THOMSON. C & WM, 32 Green, Aberdeen, 1836.

McKENZIE, ANDREW. Turriff, ABD, Late Victorian period. Wpr.- ANDREW / McKENZIE / WATCH & CLOCK MAKER / JEWELLER &c. / HIGH STREET / TURRIFF. Orn. bdr. On the back: : '7 No[v], 1901:' His son John, b. 13.6.1883, grad. MA at Aberdeen University in 1904, and became a missionary in India. He was app. Vice-Chancellor of. the University of Bombay in 1831.

McKENZIE, GUSTAVUS. WM at 99 Barron Street, Woodside, Aberdeen, 1877.

McKENZIE, JAMES. C & WM, New Pitsligo, ABD, 1877.

McKENZIE, WILLIAM. Aberchirder, BAN. Appears as a land surveyor, 1840, and by 1847 as a WM. His wife was sub-postmistress. William was a native of FIF, and d. at Long Lane, 7.2.1899, aged 96 years. He was s/o John M., land surveyor, and Margaret Clark. William m. Ann Walker, 1814-85, d/o John W., shoemaker, and Catherine Raffan. Chrn: 1. James W., baker, Newcastle-on-Tyne; 2. Catherine.

MACKIE, ALEXANDER. Adm. freeman of the Inc. of Hmm. of Banff, 1789. Prob. in business to ca. 1820.

MACKIE, ALLAN D. Insch, ABD, ca. 1890. Wpr.- ALLAN D. MACKIE / WATCHMAKER / & JEWELLER / INSCH. Str. & bkl. bdr., advertising repairs.

MACKIE, ANDREW. WM & J, adm. to the Inc. of Hmm. of Banff, 1826, paying admission fee of £24: 10s: 4d. Member until 1835.

MACKIE, ANDREW. Fraserburgh, ABD, 1837-63. Wpr.- A. MACKIE / WATCH & CLOCK / MAKER / FRASERBURGH. Fml. double bdr., inner circlet with advert for repairs.

MACKIE, JOHN. C & WM, Strichen, ABD, 1780-1824. A native of Elgin, he lived 1755-1824.

MACKIE, JOHN. C & WM, Ellon, ABD, 1820-49. Adm. to Masonic Lodge St. George, 7.10.1821. Succ. by his former appr., JAMES WALKER. John d. 1849, aged 49 years.

MACKIE, WILLIAM. CM, WM & J, Cotton, Aberdeen, 1834-35; 73 George Street, 1835-38; 51 Upperkirkgate, 1838-40; at No.67, 1840-41; 29 St. Nicholas Street, 1844-48. Absorbed the business of WILLIAM SPARK. He res. at 34 George Street, 1841; later at 6 Donald's Court, and in 1849 at 40 Union Terrace.

MACKIE, WILLIAM. Rhynie, ABD, Late Victorian period. Wpr.- Wm. MACKIE / WATCHMAKER / AND / JEWELLER / RHYNIE. Str. & bkl. bdr. advertising repairs.

McKILLIAM or McKILLICAN, JOHN. CM, WM & NIM, 53 Marischal Street, Aberdeen, 1854-55. Succ. before 1860 by ALEXANDER EASTON.

McKINNON, GEORGE B. WM & J, 60 Netherkirkgate, Aberdeen. 1875. By 1886 at 20 St. Nicholas Street. Sometime at 94 Union Street, and at 19 St. Nicholas Street. 1895-1900+.

McKIRDIE, JOHN. C & WM, 28 Woolmanhill, Aberdeen, 1845-58; at No.26, 1859-61.

MCLEOD, J. & Co. 11 Schoolhill, Aberdeen, 1846; At No.9, 1850-65. and at No.3, 1870-87. Wpr.- JOHN McLEOD / WATCH & CLOCK / MAKER / 3 SCHOOLHILL / ABERDEEN. Orn. bdr. He was b. ca. 1826.

McMILLAN, JAMES. Aberdeen, 1894-1900+. Wpr.- JAMES McMILLAN / WATCHMAKER / & JEWELLER / 131 ROSEMOUNT PLACE / ABERDEEN. Fml. bdr., with advert for repairs.

McMILLAN, PETER. CM, WM & NIM, 11 Guest Row, Aberdeen, 1824-27; Waterloo Quay, 1828-51. He resided at 12 Guestrow, 1824-40, afterwards at Princes Street. Peter d. testate, 21.5.1851, aged 49 years.

McMILLAN, WILLIAM. CM, WM & NIM, 53 Marischal Street, Aberdeen, 1844; at Regent Quay, 1845-46; and at 28 Marischal Street, 1847-50. He m. Mary Thomson, before 1849.

McMILLAN Ltd. WM & J. 151 Union Street, Aberdeen, 1896-1900+.

McMINALE, JOHN. WM, Aberdeen, 1827.

McPHERSON, CHARLES. WM & J, Auchinblae, KCD, 1877.

McROBB, WILLIAM. C & WM. Strichen, ABD, 1860.

McWILLIAM, JAMES. C & WM, Keith. BAN, ca. 1860.

McWILLIAM, JAMES. WM, Charlestown of Aberlour, nr. Dufftown, BAN, 1877.

M

MAILING, ROBERT. CK, Aberdeen, 1630.

MAITLAND, JAMES. WM & J, 14 Carmelite Street, Aberdeen, 1886; 55a Schoolhill, 1890. The local directories show Mrs James M., WM, at 7 Little Belmont Street, 1895.

MAITLAND, THOMAS. C & WM, Woodside, Aberdeen, 1820-25. He went to America where his wife, Isabella Alexander, d. 15.11.1852, aged 61.

MALCOLM, ANDREW. Appr. to JOHN FRASER, C & WM, Aberdeen, and went to Gloucester, England, to improve his skills. Commenced business at Belmont Street, Aberdeen, and took over JOHN FRASER'S business at 170 Union Street. ca. 1870. At 13 Union Place, 1885-89; and at 433 Union Street, 1890-1901. He resided at that time at 20 Esselmont Avenue, and d. unm. on 27.12.1801, aged 60 years.

MANN, JAMES. C & WM, Woodside, Aberdeen, 1828-35.

MARCH, JAMES. German CM, 42 George Street, Aberdeen, 1841-47. Sometime James and Matthew M., but James later on his own account at 13 Hutcheon Street, where he was also a spirit-dealer. Poss. the craftsman at 186 George Street, 1877.

MARCH, JOSEPH. German CM, 42 George Street, Aberdeen, 1835. Sometime Joseph M. & Co. He lived 1810-38. Bro/of THOMAS M.

MARCH, MATTHEW. German CM, 21 Queen Street, Aberdeen, 1835. Ptn., James & Matthew M., 42 George Street, 1841-47. He m. Margaret, d/o David Masson, dec. customs officer.

MARCH, MATTHEW. C & WM, Church Street, MacDuff, BAN, 1877.

MARCH, S. & Co. C & WM, Aberdeen, ca. 1820-24.

MARCH, THOMAS. German CM, Aberdeen, bro/o JOSEPH M, d. 5.10.1837, aged 26 years, and was bur. in St. Peter's Chyd., Spittal.

MARNOCH, ROBERT. Kintore, ABD, ca. 1845. Wpr.- ROBERT MARNOCH / WATCH & CLOCK / MAKER / JEWELLER &c. / KINTORE. Orn. bdr.

MARR, JAMES. Keith, BAN, ca. 1865. Wpr.- JAMES MARR / WATCHMAKER / JEWELLER / CLOCKMAKER / 145 MID STREET / KEITH. Fml. triple bdr., inner with crown at apex and advert for clock and watch repairs.

MATHERS, GEORGE. C & WM, Errol Street, Peterhead, ABD, 1820-50.

MATHEW or MATHIE, ANDREW. C & WM, Marischal Street, Peterhead, ABD, 1846- 60. Moved to Rose Street, and prob. d. before 1865.

MEARNS, ERNEST. C & WM, Banff. He m. there, 30.9.1749, Janet, d/o Mrs Guthrie of Blackhouse.

MEARNS, JOHN. C & WM, Gilcomston, Aberdeen, 1720-57. He had several chrn. between 1722 and 1745. His first wife d. in 1743, and he m. (ii) Rebecca Gibson, who later m. John Fraser, Jr., merchant in Aberdeen. John M., who was an Episcopalian, was bur. at St. Peter's Chyd., 21.3.1757.

MEARNS, JOHN. Steps of Gilcomston, Aberdeen [? 1792]-1846. At 11 Schoolhill, as C & WM, 1824-50. Prob. related to the above JOHN M. He m. at Leochel Cushnie, 25.8. 1832, Jane, d/o the dec. Alexander Moir, farmer. He ret. to Aberchirder, BAN.

MELDRUM, PETER. C & WM adm. freeman of the Inc. of Hmm. of Banff, 1812.

MELVILLE, ROBERT. CK in Aberdeen, 1645-51. He was s/o the dec. David M., stationer-B.

MELVIN, CHARLES. WM & J, Union Street, Aberdeen, 1890-1900+.

MEMESS, JAMES. CM in Garvock, KCD, ca. 1750; at Benholm, 1778, and Johnshaven, 1788, when whipped and banished for a capital offence. Poss. the WM noted at Berwick-on-Tweed, 1800-06. Prob. related to JOHN N. James m. at Edinburgh, 18.7.1778, Anne, d/o the dec. Hugh Thomson, weaver at Bervie, KCD.

MEMESS, JOHN. CM, Johnshaven KCD, ca. 1765. Prob. rel. to JAMES N.

MEMIS, WILLIAM. CM in Aberdeen, 1787

MERCER, HAY. C & WM, 25 North Street, Aberdeen, 1831; at 27 West North Street, 1837-51, and at No.87 until 1854. He had a large trade in the countryside around Aberdeen, selling watches by Breckenridge of Kilmarnock to the ploughmen, and dealing in second-hand watches. Wpr.- HAY MERCER / WATCH & CLOCK MAKER / 67 NORTH STREET, ABERDEEN. Str. & bkl. bdr. with advert for gold and silver watches. He was s/o John M., wright, and Christian Davidson, and he m. at Aberdeen, 23.12.1847, Mary Ann, d/o Thomas Best, merchant, and had issue: 1. Hay, b. ca. 1849, dy; 2. Betsy, b. ca. 1851; 3. William, b. ca. 1853; 4. John, b. ca. 1854. Hay d. of apoplexy at 27 North Street West, 1.1.1855, and was bur. at Spittal.

MERSON, JAMES. C & WM, Gordon Street, Huntly, ABD, 1837-47.

MESSMER, MICHAEL. C & WM, 95 George Street, Aberdeen, 1855-66.

MICHIE, GEORGE S. At 25 Bridge Street, Aberdeen, 1885; moved to No.27 before 1895. Wpr.- GEORGE S. MICHIE / WATCHMAKER / & JEWELLER / ABERDEEN. Faded bdr.

MIDDLETON, JOSEPH. Appr. to PETER GILL, C & WM in Aberdeen, for 5 years from 1.1.1793. Adm. to the Inc. of Hmm., 20.10.1810, and d. soon afterwards. He was s/o Francis M. in Miltoun of Culsh.

MILLAR, CHARLES. Jour. C & WM with JOHN BROWN, Aberdeen, before 1829, when he commenced business at Cotton. He d. in 1836, and his widow contd. the business for a few years.

MILLAR, WILLIAM. WM & J, 167 Union Street, Aberdeen, 1895.

MILLAR & Co. WM & J, 39 Bridge Street, Aberdeen, 1897-1900+.

MILLER, WILLIAM. C & WM, 17 St. Nicholas Street, Aberdeen, 1845-48.

MILNE, ALEXANDER. C & WM, 64 North Street, Aberdeen, 1820-39; 40 Mealmarket, 1839; 27 Mealmarket, 1840-42, residing in house above the shop.

MILNE, ALEXANDER F. Clock thus signed, Aberdeen, ca. 1820. Poss. the above craftsman.

MILNE, GEORGE. C & WM, 29 Mealmarket Lane, Aberdeen, 1846. He m. at John Knox FC, Aberdeen, Ann, d/o James Middleton, baker in Aberdeen.

MILNE, JOSEPH. C & WM, Huntly, ABD, 1797.

MILNE, ROBERT. C & WM, Queen Street, Aberdeen, 1821.

MILNE, ROBERT. WM & J, Laurencekirk, KCD, 1877.

MILNE, THOMAS. C & WM, Huntly, ABD, 1780.

MILNE & CARRY. WM & J, 57 Rosemount Viaduct, Aberdeen, 1895.

MITCHELL, ALEXANDER. WM & J, 37 Upperkirkgate, Aberdeen, 1877-1900+.

MITCHELL, JAMES. OP, W-repairer, hardware merchant and cutler, 70 Queen Street, Aberdeen, 1827; 39 East North Street, 1841, and at Shuttle Street, 1842. He m. Helen, d/o James Duncan and Isabella Black. James M. d. 29.10.1858, and she survived him.

MITCHELL, JAMES. C & WM, Inverurie, ABD, 1808.

MITCHELL, JAMES. Keith, BAN, Mid Victorian period. Wpr.- JAS. MITCHELL / WATCH / AND / CLOCKMAKER / KEITH. Orn. bdr. On the back: '28th August 1861'.

MITCHELL, JAMES. C & WM, Strichen, ABD, 1877.

MITCHELL, WILLIAM. C & WM, 32 St. Nicholas Street, Aberdeen, 1820-26. At No.44, 1827-32; Schoolhill, 1832-33; Charles Court, Upperkirkgate, 1833- 34, and later at Shiprow. He resided latterly at Long Acre.

MITCHELL, WILLIAM. C & WM, Peterhead, ABD, ca. 1858. He m. Helen, d/o James Mearns, farmer, and Susan Moir. She predeceased him, 29.12.1864, and was bur. at St. Peter's Chyd., Spittal.

MOIR, JAMES. C & WK, Aberdeen. Emigrated to Nicol Township, Wellington County, Ontario, Canada, 1835.

MORISON, THEODORE. Bridge of Dee, Aberdeen, 1846. Wpr.- THEDORE *[sic]* MORISON / WATCH AND CLOCK MAKER / BRIDGE OF DEE. Wide bdr. with ryme above and below the above details.

MORRISON, GEORGE. C & WM, Aberdeen, before 1779, when his son JOHN M. was appr. to him. He made longcase clocks in association with JAMES BONNAR. George d. ca. 1792.

MORRISON, JOHN. Appr. to his father, GEORGE M., 26.2.1779. In business, ca.1786-1840. He was bur. at. St. Machar's Chyd., 16.1.1841.

MORRISON, ROBERT. C & WM, 35 Upperkirkgate, Aberdeen, 1858-68, in succ. to HUGH DIVORLY. At 60 Nethergate, 1869-75.

MORRISON & SKAKLE. CM, WM & J, 65 Netherkirkgate, Aberdeen, 1877-90.

MORTIMER, GEORGE. Jour. WM, Portsoy, BAN, d. 1882, aged 19 years.

MORTIMER, JAMES. C & WM, Cullen, BAN, ca. 1795. He was b. 29.12.1767. s/o Alexander M., miller, Newmiln of Cullen, and Margaret Murie. He was bro/o WILLIAM M., and by his wife Jane Bremner, had a son WILLIAM.

MORTIMER, WILLIAM. Bro/of the above JAMES M., and in business at Lower Castle Street, BAN, before 1837. Wpr.- Female figure representing 'Hope', holding an anchor in the dexter hand; the sinister resting on a shield lettered: Wm. MORTIMER / WATCH & CLOCK / MAKER / CULLEN. Orn. bdr. On the back: " 15 Feb. 1838". He was sometime at Old Cullen before moving to Lower Castle Street. William m. Elizabeth Drum, from Gamrie parish.

MORTIMER, WILLIAM. C & WM, Boyndie, BAN, before 1830, and moved to Portsoy before 1837. In his later years, when there was fierce competition from imported clocks and watches, he made fine tools, brass plates for coffins, and was a general dealer. William was s/o JAMES M. and Jane Bremner, and b.1.1.1801. He m. Jane Riddock, 1821-1915, and had issue: 1. GEORGE jour. WM, d. 8.3. 1882; 2. William, resided at Sand End, Portsoy. The CM d. at 18 Seafield Street, Portsoy, 12.3.1882.

MOWAT, JOHN. CM, locksmith and bell-founder, Old Aberdeen. Adm. to the Inc. of Hmm. there, 1717, and became a trade-B, 13.6.1719. He had an extensive business. The bell-making part of his business descended to his former appr., ANDREW LAWSON, ca. 1746.

MUNRO, G.W. WM & J, 5 Woolmanhill, Aberdeen, 1880. By 1886 appears as G.W. Munro & Co., 3 Gilcomston Steps. The local 1895 *Directory* shows G.W. Munro, 166 Holburn Street.

MUNRO, MALCOLM. WM & J, 161 Gallowgate, Aberdeen, 1877; 33 George Street, 1880-88.

MUNRO, WILLIAM. C & WM, 49 Spittal, Old Aberdeen, 1841-46.

MURISON, CHARLES. Strichen, ABD, ca. 1890. Wpr.- On a shield: CHARLES MURISON / WATCHMAKER / STRICHEN. Fml. bdr., inner circlet advertising repairs to clocks, watches and jewellery, and intimating that he stocked violin strings.

MURISON, GEORGE. C & WM, Mintlaw, Old Deer, ABD, 1850-80. He was b. 18-32, s/o William M., stonemason, and Elspet Reid. George m. in 1874, Isabella, d/o James Whyte, quarrier. He d. at Mintlaw, 23.10.1880.

MURISON, GEORGE. WM & J, Mid Street, Fraserburgh, ABD, 1877-1919. In 1877 he commenced business at Mid Street, having served his appr. with CHARLES GRAY. For a time he had his son JAMES ROSS M. as a ptn. An active free-mason, he was a founder member and treasurer of the local golf club, and sometime president of Fraserburgh Bowling Club. Wpr.- G. MURISON / WATCH MAKER / & / JEWELLER / BANK BUILDINGS / 3 MID STREET / FRASERBURGH. Orn. str. & bkl. bdr., with advert for repairs. George was s/o George M., dairy man, and Charlotte Ironside. He m. Maggie Ross. Besides his son JAMES Ross M., he had a son Alfred Ross M., rector of Thurso Academy.

MURISON, JAMES ROSS. Fraserburgh, ABD, ca. 1900+. Wpr.- Armorial bearings quartered, but indistict, with a cock as crest and angels as supporters. Above the shield appears: J.R. MURISON / WATCHMAKER / JEWELLER / 64 BROAD STREET / FRASERBURGH. Plain bdr., with advert for watches, clocks and jewellery. He was s/o GEORGE M. and Maggie Ross. His daughter Helen, b. 30.12.1921, graduated MA at Aberdeen, 1955.

MURRAY, JOHN. CM, WM & NIM. Adm. to the Inc. of Hmm. of Aberdeen, 29.12. 1827, and became a Trade-B, 19.5.1828. At Quay, 1824-27; St. Nicholas Street, 1827-28; 37 Quay, 1828-39; 30 Broadford, 1839-40; 36 Quay, 1840- 42. Listed as a Parliamentary voter, 1841. Resided in 1831 at 37 Quay, later at No.30. Wpr.- JOHN MURRAY / WATCH & CLOCK / MAKER / ABERDEEN. Bdr. trimmed to fit small watch. On the back, "24 May 1826".

MURRAY, WILLIAM. WM & J, Market Gallery, Aberdeen, 1877.

MUTCH, ALEXANDER. Self-taught WM in Ellon, ABD, 1841-71. He was s/o James M., labourer, and ---- Norrie. Alexander m. Isabella, d/o Alexander Brown and ---- Connon. They had, with other issue: 1. John; 2. Mrs Crighton, New Deer. The WM d. 18.3.1873, aged 76 years.

MUTCH, GEORGE. C & WM, Ellon, ABD, ca. 1860-85. Prob. related to the above ALEXANDER M. His widow was alive at London in 1925. A mahogany longcase clock by George, with white dial, the four seasons in the corners and Burns at the plough in the arch, was noted by Lawrance. George was succ. by GEORGE SHEPHERD.

N

NICOL, R.W. WM & J, 115 Union Street, Aberdeen, 1886.

NICOL, WILLIAM. WM, Fyvie, ABD, 1868-75. He was s/o John M., farmer in Blackbog, and Sarah Littlejohn. William m. 11.8.1869, Janel b. ca. 1846, d/o James Wilkie and Catherine Peter. They emigrated to New Zealand in 1875, with their chrn. : 1. William; 2. Alexander; 3. Catherine.

NIVEN, ALEXANDER. C & WM, Kincardine O'Neil and Torphins, ABD, 1877.

O

OGG & McMILLAN. CM, WM & NIM, 53 Marischal Street, Aberdeen, 1844-45; at 30 Regent Quay, 1845-47. The ptn. was prob. WILLIAM McMILLAN, of Shiprow. William Ogg m. 22.1.1846, Isabellal d/o James Kelman, overseer at Broadford. They resided in Wales Street.

OGSTON, GEORGE. C & WM, 65 Union Street, Aberdeen, 1824-26. He resided at 1 Marischal Street.

P

PARK, GEORGE. CM, WM & J, Fishcross Street, Fraserburgh, ABD, 1836, previously at Craigellie, Lonmay, ABD. He m. his cousin, Jean, d/o James Park, tailor in Fraserburgh, and Elizabeth Lawrance. She d. 12.6.1877, aged 78 years. Two chrn. d. in nonage. George d. 1.3.1840.

PARK, JAMES. C & WM, Kilmacolm, RFW, 1802.

PARK, JAMES. C & WM, Inverurie, ABD, before 1842. May have worked for a time in Aberdeen. He made longcase clocks which played popular tunes. He was poss. related to JOHN P.

PARK, JOHN. C & WM, Inverurie, ABD, 1837. Signed his longcase clocks: "Jn. PARK, INVERURY".

PATERSON, GEORGE. C & WM, Hutcheon Street, Aberdeen, 1831-32; 70 Causwayend, 1833-36; Cotton, 1836-37. Appears as George F. Paterson & Co., at Woodside, 1837-38. At 114 George Street, 1838-39.

PATERSON, JAMES. C & WM, Banff, 1779-1829. Owned a house in High Street, 1823. Adm. B & G of Banff, 14.6.1779, "on account of the singular regard the magistrates bear him". He was b. at Mill of Durn, Fordyce, 21.4.1757, and m. Janet, d/o Bailie Patrick Cassie, by his wife Janet Bisset. James d. in October, 1829.

PAUL, JAMES. WM & J, 15 Haddon Street, Woodside, Aberdeen, 1877.

PETRIE, JOHN. Appr. to JAMES ARGO, Peterhead, ABD, and worked for a time as jour. with JOHN GARTLY, Aberdeen. Commenced business at New Deer, ca. 1800. He was b. at Mains of Crichie, Old Deer, s/o John P. and Mary Stephen. John m. Miss Craighead, with issue, and d. 9.2.1863. Son WILLIAM was his ptn., 1840-60.

PETRIE, WILLIAM. C & WM, New Deer, as ptn. of his father, 1840-60, and after his father's retiral, on his own account. His business suffered in the 1880's owing to the importation of cheap clocks from USA. William m. Margaret Gerrie, 1820-89, a native of Monquhitter. He d. 18.3.1889, leaving issue.

PHINN, GEORGE. WM & J, 1A, Drums Lane, Aberdeen, 1890. By 1885 appears as G.W. Phinn & Co.

PHINN, WILLIAM. WM & J, 9 Drums Lane, Aberdeen, 1886-95. Prob. related to GEORGE P. Son WILLIAM, Jr.

PHINN, WILLIAM, Jr. WM & J, 28 Upperkirkgate, Aberdeen, 1886.

PIRRIE, GEORGE. CM, WM & J, Cullen, BAN, 1866-86. He lived 1841-86.

PIRRIE, JAMES. CM in Cullen, BAN, 1866-80. He was bred a cabinet-maker, and received some training from P. WILSON, in Keith, which he turned to good account. James was a man of extraordinary ability, erecting, among others, a town clock at Banff, and he made longcase clocks. Other interests incl. photography, dentistry, and music. By his wife, Margaret Riach, 1812-92, from Enzie, he had chrn: 1. GEORGE, noted above; 2. James, b. 1844, graduated MA at Aberdeen, 1865, and became assistant master at the City of London School; 3. Ann, b. 1847, m. Richard Bellingham, of Beccles, Suffolk. The WM was s/o George P., farmer in Cranach, nr. Keith, and d. at Cullen, 22.7.1881.

PROCTOR, JAMES. C & WM, Tarland, ABD, ca. 1855. He also farmed at Braerodach, Cromar, and in 1879 purchased Kirkville, Skene. James m. Ann, d/o William Hector, and d. 31.1.1888.

R

RAE, JOHN. C & WM, adm. freeman of the Inc. of Hmm. of Aberdeen, 1816, and entered as B the same year. At 45 Union Street, 1824. He resided then at 9 Innes Lane, later at Northfield, Gilcomston.

RAMAGE, CHARLES. C & WM, Aberdeen, 1852-59. He resided at Regent Quay in 1852, when he took as ptn., CHARLES SMITH. Charles d. 12.4.1859.

RAMSAY, GEORGE. CR, Old Machar, ABD, 1646.

RANNIE, ALEXANDER. C & WM, Turriff, ABD, 1836.

REID, JOHN. CM in Banff. Repaired the town clock in 1721, and in May, 1724, installed a new one at a cost of £80: 10s. Scots. His wife was Jean Fraser, who d. 6.9.1722.

REID, JONATHAN. WM & J, Northfield, Aberdeen, ca. 1865. He d. at Windy Wynd, and was bur. at St. Peter's Chyd., Spittal, 24.10.1874, aged 45. Jonathan was s/o Peter R., wincy weaver, and Jean Bremner. He m. Jean Black, who survived him.

REID, PATRICK. Tarland and Strathdon, ABD, 1893. Wpr.- PATRICK REID / WATCH MAKER / & JEWELLER / TARLAND & / STRATHDON. Str. & bkl. bdr. with advert for repairs.

REID, WILLIAM. WM, Aberdeen, poss. jour. Bur. at St. Peter's Chyd., Spittal, 11.12.1853, aged 34 years.

REITH, JOHN. Blacksmith & CR at Banchory-Devenick, ABD, ca. 1820-38. He made at least one longcase clock. John d. at Hilldowntree, 1.3.1838, aged 41 years. A son of the same name was b. 1828.

RENNIE, ALEXANDER. C & WM, Turriff, ABD, ca. 1835. Poss. the craftsman at Insch, 1847-48.

RETTIE, M. & SON. Aberdeen, 1828-90. Middleton R. and his son James may not have been time-served watchmakers, but the father was described as a jeweller. They had a thriving business at 111, later 151 Union Street, retailing clocks, watches, silver and plated ware, jewellery. rings, lamps, bronze household ornaments, cutlery and fancy goods. Their japanned work was executed by ALEXANDER HAY. James d. 10.2.1896, aged 83 years. He was the author of *Aberdeen fifty years ago* (Aberdeen, 1868, repr. 1972).

RIDDEL, D. & J. WM & J, Aberdeen. Donaldson and James, sons of Donaldson R., wright-B, and Margaret Bennie, were in business at St. Nicholas Street from ca. 1840. Wpr.- D. & J. RIDDEL / WATCH MAKERS / AND JEWELLERS / 45 St. NICHOLAS STREET / ABERDEEN. Str. & bkl. bdr., advertising watches. They moved temporarily to 125 Union Street, and were at Riddel's Court Windmill Brae, before 1843. Moved to 72 Broad Street, 1844, and to 43 St. Nicholas Street, 1852. James appears to have separated from the firm about this time, and d. at Peterculter, 17.6.1859, aged 46 years. Donaldson was at 33 Charlotte Street, 1877. He m. (i) Jane, 1803-74, d/o Robert Carnegie and Janet Reid; (ii) 1876, Christian Jeffrey, 1824-88. Donaldson d. at 8 Kingsland Place, 20.3.1883, aged 72 years.

RIDDEL, ROBERT. C & WM, Old Meldrum, ABD, ca. 1825-43. Prob. related to CHARLES R. He m. Mary Mann, 1791-1853, and had issue: 1. Charles, 1816-46, ironmonger; 2. James Mann, 1825-56, ironmonger. Robert d. in 1844, aged 53 years.

RIDDELL, W.A. Echt, ABD, ca. 1890. Wpr.- W.A. RIDDELL / WATCHMAKER / ECHT. Str. & bkl. bdr. advertising repairs.

ROBB, WILLIAM J. Inverurie, ABD, ca. 1895. Wpr.- [In MS., 614] / Wm. ROBB / PRACTICAL / WATCHMAKER / HIGH STREET / INVERURIE. Str. & bkl. bdr., with advert for repairs.

ROBERTSON, ALEXANDER. C & WM, Aberdeen, 1815-23. He had a child bur. in St. Peter's Chyd., Spittal, 4.3.1817. In 1822 he subscribed for a copy of John Leslie's *Interesting Anecdotes,* published at Aberdeen.

ROBERTSON, DAVID. CK, Aberdeen, 1607-08, along with ADAM GORDON.

ROBERTSON, JAMES. C & WM, Auchinblae, KCD, 1877.

ROBERTSON, JOHN. WM in Aberdeen, 1835; poss. a jour. He m. 4.12.1835, Margaret, d/o William Brown, tailor in Elgin.

ROBERTSON, JOHN. WM & J, Market Gallery, Aberdeen, 1880-96, sometime as J. Robertson & Co.

ROBERTSON, WILLIAM. Appr. to GEORGE MUTCH, C & WM, Ellon, ABD, and worked as a jour. with GEORGE SHEPHERD there, before commencing business on his own account at Leven, FIF, before 1890. He was s/o John R., slater in Ellon.

ROBSON, WILLIAM. C & WM, Banff, 1860-77.

RODGERS, WILLIAM. Stonehaven, KCD, 1820-60. Wpr.- WILL^m. RODGERS / WATCH & CLOCK / MAKER / STONEHAVEN. Fml. Bdr., with advert for engraving, jewellery, wedding rings and repairs.

ROMBACH, JOSEPH & Co. C & WM, 74 King Street, Aberdeen, 1860.

ROSE, ALEXANDER. WM in Aberdeen, 1846, poss. a jour. Witness, 25.8.1846, at the m. of JOHN FREDERICK and Elizabeth Mollison.

ROSS, ALEXANDER. Jour. WM in Aberdeen, d. 29.5.1843, aged 18 years. Bur. in St. Peter's Chyd., Spittal.

ROSS, JAMES. Huntly, ABD, ca. 1865-95. Wpr.- JAMES ROSS / PRACTICAL / WATCH MAKER / DUKE STREET / HUNTLY. Orn. bdr., with advert for repairs.

ROSS, JAMES. C & WM, New Deer, ABD, 1877.

ROSS, PETER. WM & J, Aberdeen, bur. at St. Peter's Chyd., Spit tal, 4.1.1822, aged 31 years.

ROSS, WILLIAM. A native of Banff, he was appr. to JOHN GARTLY, C & WM in Aberdeen, ca. 1811. He commenced business at Huntly, ABD, ca. 1819, and followed the methods of his old master. He went into semi-retirement, ca. 1859, but made clocks which he exported to Australia, to which country a son had emigrated. William was b. ca. 1794, and m. Jean Turpie, with chrn: 1. Jane, b. 6.12.1820; 2. Rev. William, 1821-99, MA, Marischal College, 1840, emigrated to South Australia, 1846; 3. Elizabeth, b. ca. 1823; 4. Susan, b. 13.3.1825; 5. Margaret Allan, 1826-56; 6. David, b. 11.7.1828; 7. James, b. 24.4.1830; 8. John, b. 11.2.1832; 9. Mary, b. 11.7.1833; 10. Charles Gordon, b. 1.7.1834. William d. at Chester before 1880.

ROSS, WILLIAM. C & WM, Stonehaven, KCD, 1846.

ROSS & MILLER. C & WM, 23 St. Nicholas Street, Aberdeen, 1870.

ROWEL, BENJAMIN. C & WM, 6 Correction Wynd, Aberdeen, 1845-47. Re-appears at 157 George Street, 1860-68. At No.173 by 1887, and at 2 Stafford Street, 1895.

ROWEL, JOHN. C & WM, 186 George Street, Aberdeen, 1877.

S

SANGSTER, ALEXANDER. C & WM, Sandend, Whinnyfield, Cruden, ABD, 1820-50, and did some farming. He was s/o John S., farmer, and his wife Barbara, and m. Jean Tait. Alexander d. at Sandend, 1.8.1857, testate, and aged 77 years. Son JAMES S.

SANGSTER, ALEXANDER. C & WM, Rose Street, Peterhead, ABD, 1837.

SANGSTER, JAMES. WM & farmer, Stockbridge of Bruxie, Old Deer, ABD. He was s/o ALEXANDER S. and his wife Barbara, and b. ca. 1820. In business ca. 1850-80. He m. Elizabeth, sist/o Rev. Robert Gray, Marischal College, Aberdeen. James d. 20.11.1901, and his son Alexander succ. him in the farm.

SANGSTER, SMITH & Co. C & WM, 78 Union Street, Aberdeen, 1876-78. Became Sangster & DUNNINGHAM, same address, but re-organised by 1886, when trading as WILLIAM DUNNINGHAM & Co.

SCOTT, ALEXANDER H. Market Street, Inverurie, ABD, 1900+. Wpr. -A. H. SCOTT / WATCHMAKER / AND / JEWELLER / INVERURIE / WEDDING RINGS. Double str. & bkl. bdr., inner advertising repairs. Apparently d. before 1921, when his widow was carrying on the business.

SCOTT, GEORGE. WM & J, 207 George Street, Aberdeen, 1880. At No.26 in 1886; No.102 by 1895, and at 3 Schoolhill, 1900+.

SCOTT, WILLIAM. C & WM at Aberdeen before 1798; sometime in London, and afterwards at Falkirk and Hardgate, Aberdeen. The *Commissariot Record of Aberdeen*, 22.11.1798, when his testament was confirmed, describes him as "sometime watchmaker in London, afterwards at Fallside *(sic)*, and thereafter at Hardgate of Aberdeen".

SETON, JAMES. WM & J, 187 George Street, Aberdeen, 1886-87. At 92 Maberly Street before 1900.

SHEPHERD, GEORGE. Succ. GEORGE MUTCH at Ellon, ABD, ca. 1885. Wpr.- GEORGE SHEPHERD / WATCH MAKER / & JEWELLER / BRIDGE STREET / ELLON. Str. & bkl. bdr., with advert for repairs.

SHEPHERD, GEORGE. WM & J, 55-56 Market Gallery, Aberdeen, ca. 1895-1900+.

SHERRIFF, ALEXANDER. Jour. J with William Jamieson, Aberdeen, 1828-42, but seems also to have been a WM. He resided at 34 St. Andrew Street, later at Guest Row.

SHIACH, ROBERT. CM at Torphins, ABD, ca. 1780. Prob. the craftsman who was sometime in Nova Scotia, Canada. He d. 1785, survived by a lady who may have been his second wife.

SIEVEWRIGHT, J. Aberdeen, ca. 1895. Wpr.- S. SIEVEWRIGHT / WATCHMAKER / & JEWELLER / 19 / UPPERKIRKGATE / ABERDEEN. Double str. & bkl. bdr., the inner with advert for repairs to clocks, watches and jewellery.

SIM, ALEXANDER. C & WM, Upperkirkgate, Aberdeen, ca. 1790-1818. Sometime ptn. of ROBERT WARDEN.

SIM, CHARLES. Insch, ABD, ca. 1890. Wpr.- On a shield: CHARLES SIM / WATCHMAKER / JEWELLER & CUTLER / INSCH. Fml. bdr.

SIM, JAMES. C & WM, Banff, ca. 1810, poss. the craftsman previously at Cullen, BAN. Wpr.- JAMES SIM / CLOCK & WATCH / MAKER / BANFF. Orn. bdr.

SIM, JOHN. C & WM, Banff, 1807-23.

SIM, JOHN. C & WM, Longside, ABD, 1810-65. An elder of the Free Church there, formed in 1843. He m. (i) Grace Fraser, with issue; (ii) Agnes Young, 1819-1901. John d. 27.4.1893, aged 75 years.

SIM, M. C & WM, Aberdeen, ca. 1800.

SIM & WARDEN. C & WM, Upperkirkgate, Aberdeen, ca. 1820. The ptns. were ALEXANDER SIM and ROBERT WARDEN.

SIMMERS, ROBERT G. Peterhead, ABD, 1885-95. Wpr.- ROBERT G. SIMMERS / WATCHMAKER / JEWELLER, &c./ 4 LONGATE / PETERHEAD. Orn. bdr. , with advert for wedding rings, watches, clocks, jewellery and spectacles.

SIMPSON, ALEXANDER. Fraserburgh, ABD, ca. 1863-1903. Wpr.- ALEX^R. SIMPSON / WATCH & CLOCK / MAKER / JEWELLER, &c. / 38 BROAD STREET / FRASERBURGH. Plain bdr., with regulating instructions. He was s/o William S., farmer, and Margaret Barron. Alexander m. Jane Kidd McBeath, a niece of ALEXANDER McBEATH, C & WM, Fraserburgh. He was well-known in Masonic

Circles and sometime Qm-Sgt. in the Fraserburgh Artillery. Alexander d. 4.7.1903, aged 69 years.

SIMPSON, WILLIAM & JOHN. Banff, ca. 1875. Wpr.- W^M. & JH^N. SIMPSON / WATCHMAKERS / GOLD & SILVERSMITHS / BANFF. Escrolls on mantling lettered SEALS * KEYS * CHAINS * GOLD RINGS.

SKAKLE, GEORGE. Prob. ptn., MORRISON & SKAKLE, Aberdeen, 1877-90, but on his own account at 15 Correction Wynd, 1890-96.

SMITH, ALEXANDER. C & WM, Keithhall, later at West High Street, Inverurie, ABD. In business ca. 1846-83. He erected a town clock at Inverurie, 1879. It had been made by JOHN BLACK, Aberdeen, in 1848. Alexander was burgh treasurer for 17 years. He was s/o GEORGE SMITH, Huntly, and Margaret Simpson, 1817-83. Alexander d. 1.10.1883, and was succ. by his nephew, ALEXANDER JOHN SMITH.

SMITH, ALEXANDER. C & WK, Turriff, ABD, ca. 1830-78. He was s/o James S. and Margaret Grieve, and d. unm. 26.11.1878, aged 63 years. His sister Annie, m. JAMES GAMMACK.

SMITH, ALEXANDER JOHN. C & WM, Inverurie, ABD, 1883-1900+. Succ. to the business of his uncle, ALEXANDER S. It has been stated that he never made clocks except under his uncle's supervision, but his name appears on dials. He ret. to Aberdeen, ca. 1918. His wife was Frances Cockburn, who d. 11. 11.1920, aged 63 years.

SMITH, A. & J. WM & J, OP and retailers of scientific optical instruments, Netherkirkgate, Aberdeen, 1867. Moved to 25 St. Nicholas Street, 1866. At No.23, 1876. Also at 113 Union Street, 1879, and at No. 1895-1900+. The senior ptn. Alexander, was b. ca. 1835, s/o Alexander S., shoemaker, and Isabella Donald. He was adm. to the Inc. of Hmm. 5.11.1877, his essay having been a gold wedding ring and the setting of a brooch. He m. Catherine Nicoll, with issue a son Alexander George, and d. testate in 1904. His younger brother and ptn., John S., was b. ca. 1844, and adm. to the Inc. of Hmm., 4.6.1880, his essay having been the same as Alexander's. He m. Ann Brown, Widow Helm, and had at least two sons, Harold and Alfred. John d. testate in 1911. His son Alfred and his cousin Alexander George, carried on the business.

SMITH, CHARLES. CM, CRM & WM, 30 Regent Quay, Aberdeen, 1843-45; at St. James Quay, 1846-49; 49 Regent Quay, 1850. Adm. to the Inc. of Hmm. 28. 12.1843, and as a Trade-B, 12.1.1844. He had as ptn., ca. 1851-59, CHARLES RAMAGE. Charles S. resided at 14 Wellington Street, and he m. Margaret Robertson, who d. 21.12.1855, aged 37. He d. 27.4.1862, and was bur. in St. Clement's Chyd. Surgeon-Major John Grant, in Corfu, Ionian Islands, Greece, was served heir of provision general to him, 21.7.1863.

SMITH, GEORGE. C & WM, Gordon Street, Huntly. ABD, ca. 1820-46; later in Inverurie. He was s/o James S., tanner, poss. in Brechin, and Janet Simpson. George m. Isabella Fraser, 1787-1868, and had issue: 1. JAMES, WM in Inverurie; 2. ALEXANDER, WM, Keithhall. George d. at Inverurie, 22.6.1856, aged 68 years.

SMITH, GEORGE. C & WM, Muir of Rhynie, ABD, ca. 1845.

SMITH, GEORGE B. Ellon, ABD, ca. 1897-1900+. Wpr.- GEORGE B. SMITH / WATCHMAKER / & JEWELLER / BRIDGE STREET / ELLON. Str. & bkl. bdr., with advert for repairs.

SMITH, JAMES. C & WM, Aberdeen, before 1860 to 1890. Worked as a jour. in Coventry, and with William Harvey, C & WM, Stirling. Poss. in business for a short period at Inverurie, but became a ptn. of DAVID GILL, Aberdeen, before 1860. On his own account at 18 St. Nicholas Street, 1865. Moved to 20 Belmont Street, where in 1877 he was a Ws. dealer in horological tools and materials. At 37 Market Gallery, 1880, and took as ptn, his son WILLIAM ALEXANDER S. James was b. ca. 1816, s/o GEORGE S., Huntly. and Isabella Fraser. He m. (i) before 1846, Marion Wilson, and had issue; (ii) Elizabeth Clark.

SMITH, JAMES & SON. C & WM, Aberdeen. Commenced business before 1860, at 37 Market Gallery. Son WILLIAM ALEXANDER S. became ptn.

SMITH, JOHN. C & WM. Peterhead, ABD, ca. 1790.

SMITH, JOHN. C & WM. Inverurie, ABD, ca. 1830.

SMITH, JOHN A. C & WM, 2 Broad Street, Peterhead, ABD, 1877.

SMITH, JOHN A. & SON. Peterhead, ABD, ca. 1880. The above JOHN S. and a son. Wpr.- JOHN A. SMITH & SON / WATCH / AND / CLOCK MAKER / PETERHEAD. Plain bdr. with advert for clocks, watches, jewellery and barometers.

SMITH, WALTER. CM in Aberdeen, 1790-1802. Adm. to the Inc. of Hmm. of Aberdeen, 26.4.1791. He was s/o Patrick S., B of Aberdeen. Walter m. Ann, d/o Murdoch Macfarlane, schoolmaster at Glentanner, without issue. She was widowed before 1803, and d. 1834.

SMITH, WILLIAM. CM in Aberdeen, 1700.

SMITH, WILLIAM. Buckie, BAN, prob. Mid and Late Victorian periods. Wpr.- WILLIAM SMITH / WATCH MAKER / JEWELLER & / OPTICIAN / BUCKIE. Str. & bkl. bdr., with advert for repairs. On the back: "29.5.99".

SMITH, WILLIAM ALEXANDER. Ws. C & WM, and dealer in watch materials and tools, 37 Market Gallery, Aberdeen. Ptn. with his father, JAMES S., and succ. to the business.

SMITH & RAMAGE. NIM, C & WM, 45 Regent Quay, Aberdeen, 1852-61. The ptns. were CHARLES SMITH and CHARLES RAMAGE.

SMOUTS, JOHN GEORGE. German CM, Banchory-Ternan, KCD, d. 22.10.1863, aged 54 years.

SPARK, WILLIAM. C & WM, Aberdeen, 1806-46. Adm. freeman of the Inc. of Hmm. there, 15.9.1806, and entered as Trade-B, 21.9.1813. Deacon of the Hmm., 1823. In business at Marischal Street, 1820-30; 29 St. Nicholas Street, 1831-46. Prob. ret. in 1846, and moved from his home in Shiprow to his property of Craigiepark. William was b. ca. 1774, s/o Thomas S., Clerk and Treasurer of Aberdeen Infirmary. He m. Helen Esson, who d. 27.12.1868, aged 78 years. The CM d. 15.3.1870, and was bur. at Aboyne. His gr-neph. Thomas Spark Sinclair, 1838-1906, Advocate in Aberdeen, adopted the surname of Spark in 1870, on succ. to half of his moveable property.

SPEKULAND, M. & Co. WM & J, Flourmill Lane, Aberdeen, 1890. He had also business interests in Edinburgh.

SPENCE, HUGH. Appr. to GEORGE SMITH. CM in Huntly, prob. ca. 1810, and may have worked for a time as his jour. Commenced business on his own account at Gordon Street, Huntly, before 1830. Moved to Alford after 1837. Wpr.- HUGH SFENCE / WATCH & CLOCK / MAKER / ALFORD. Orn. bdr. He was s/o David S., auctioneer, and Helen Stewart. Hugh d. at Hollybank, Alford, 12.7.1883. aged 88 years.

SPENCE, JOHN. At Longside, ABD, Late Victorian period. Wpr.- JOHN SPENCE / WATCHMAKER / AND / JEWELLER / LONGSIDE. Str. & bkl. bdr., with advert for repairs. On the back: "July, 1898".

STEPHANI, JOHN. German CM & OP, 68 Broad Street, Aberdeen, 1845-46.

STEPHEN, CHARLES. WM & J, Old Meldrum, ABD, 1837-63.

STEPHEN, CHARLES. At Peterhead, ABD, 1868-1900+. Wpr.- CHARLES STEPHEN / WATCH MAKER / AND / JEWELLER / 5 BROAD STREET / PETERHEAD. Double fml. bdr., inner advertising wedding rings, repairs and cleaning of watches. Another wpr. describes him also as a SS.

STEPHEN, DAVID. WM & J, Johnshaven, KCD, 1839.

STEPHEN, JAMES. C & WM, Old Meldrum, ABD, 1837-60. Poss. related to CHARLES S.

STEVENSON, JAMES. WM, J & optical instrument maker, 24 Wellington Place, Aberdeen, 1885; at Schoolhill by 1887, and moved to 31 Ashvale Place by 1890. In 1900 at 36 Holburn Street.

STEVENSON, JOHN. WM & J, 8 Schoolhill, Aberdeen, 1893-1900+.

STILL, WILLIAM. C & WM, Gelleymill Street, MacDuff, Banff, 1846. John Smith errs in placing him in Aberdeen.

STRAUB, B. C & WM, 18 George Street, Aberdeen, 1870.

SUTHERLAND, DAVID. C & WM, Keith, BAN, 1803-25. He was a director of the Keith Friendly Society, 1803. He d. ca. 1830, aged 70 years.

SUTHERLAND, GEORGE. CM, WM & J, Stonehaven, KCD, 1830.

SUTHERLAND, JAMES. A self-taught CM at New Machar, ABD, who made his own dials and cases, ca. 1825-55. He also made wooden bowls and spoons. James was s/o William S., carpenter, and Elizabeth Hunter. He m. Catherine Brownie, and d. 15.7.1855, aged 62.

T

TAYLOR, ALEXANDER. WM in Aberdeen, poss. a jour. His wife, Margaret Simpson, was bur. in St. Peter's Chyd., Spittal, 7.5.1841, aged 30.

TAYLOR, G. WM & J, 25 Woolmanhill, Aberdeen, 1880, in the the premises vacated by MALCOLM MUNRO.

TAYLOR, JAMES. C & WM, Strichen, ABD, 1799-1836. It has been stated that his true surname was Douglas, and that he had to leave London during political disturbances. His ancestors prob. hailed from Perth. He d. 12.11.1846, aged 90. Son JOSEPH T.

TAYLOR, JOSEPH. C & WM, Strichen, ABD, 1837. He was s/o JAMES T., and d. 1851, aged 57 years.

TELFER, ALEXANDER. Sometime CM in Aberdeen, d. in Antigua, 1806.

THEMAN, DAVID. Aberdeen, 1457-1503. "Keeper of the common horeloge and knock" of Aberdeen, engraved the city arms on badges made for the minstrels who were to play at the wedding of James IV, and Princess Margaret (Tudor) of England, in 1503. Each contained 1½ ounces of silver. JAMES KEMP was appr. to him in 1457, so prob. in business before that year. In 1493 he made an agreement to uphold the common clock of Aberdeen. David may have succ. JOHNE CRUKSHANKE, the earliest known name in Scottish horology.

THOMPSON, JAMES T. Active 1872-1900. At 17 St. Nicholas Street, Aberdeen, 1872-87. Moved to Kintore, ABD, ca. 1890, and to Kirkcaldy, FIF, 1900. Wpr.- JAMES T. THOMPSON / PRACTICAL WATCH / & CLOCK MAKER / JEWELLER &c./ KINTORE. Str, & bkl. bdr. On the back: "April 1895". He d. at Kirkcaldy, 24.12.1903.

THOMPSON, J.W. At Peterhead, ABD, ca. 1895. Wpr.- J.W. THOMPSON / WATCH- MAKER / AND / JEWELLER / 5 BROAD STREET / PETERHEAD. In escrolls: SEALS, KEYS * CHAINS / GOLD RINGS.

THOMSON, ALEXANDER. CM in Banff, adm. to the Domestic Society of Keith, 12.7.1736.

THOMSON, A.S. WM & J, 113 Holburn Street, Aberdeen, 1898-1900+.

THOMSON, GEORGE. C & WM, Inverurie, ABD, 1816-45. May have succ. WILLIAM LUNDIE. He made good longcase clocks. George is thought to have gone abroad.

THOMSON, JAMES. C & WM, Old Aberdeen, 1670-1706; Montrose, ANS, 1706-31. He sold a "pendall clock w[h]ilk goes 24 hours", poss. second-hand, to James Rickart, 1671-1749, merchant in Aberdeen, 16.5.1705. The same party paid him £54 Scots, 17.12.1705, for "a pendal silver watch". He was app. keeper of the church clock of St. Machar's Cathedral, 5.12.1700, at a salary of 10 merks yearly. The Kirk-Session paid him £2: 1s: 6d Scots, in 1702, for "a tow to hing the clok pace". He worked in Montrose for 25 years. James m. Margaret Nicolson. Their chrn. incl. : 1. Anne, bapt. 27.6. 1699; 2. Jean, bapt. 17.11.1700.

THOMSON, JAMES 0. Fraserburgh, ABD, ca. 1805. Wpr.- JAMES 0. THOMSON / WATCH MAKER / & JEWELLER / 67 CROSS STREET / FRASERBURGH. Str. & bkl. bdr., with advert for repairs.

THOMSON, JOHN. C & WM, Aberdeen, Early Victorian period. He d. before 6.8.1860, when his brother, Matthew T., upholsterer in Edinburgh, was served heir in special in two feus of the Calsay Croft of Aberdeen.

THOMSON, JOSEPH. WM & J, 5 Broad Street, Peterhead, ABD, ca. 1880.

THOMSON, ROBERT. At 42½ Upperkirkgate, Aberdeen, 1873; No. 34½, 1885-1900. Wpr.- R. THOMSON / WATCHMAKER / AND JEWELLER / 34½ UPPER KIRKGATE / ABERDEEN. Str. & bkl. bdr., with advert for repairs. A later wpr. of the same design, ca. 1923, shows the business being carried on by G.F. Bruce and W.A. Kemp, at 27 George Street.

THOMSON, WILLIAM. Methlick, ABD, poss. before 1900. Wpr. of Late Victorian design: Wm. THOMSON / WATCH MAKER / METHLICK. Str. & bkl. bdr., within a wreath of roses and lettered *Watches & jewellery of every description carefully repaired.*

TOCHER & MITCHELL. Aberdeen, Late Georgian and Early Regency periods. Wpr.- TOCHER & MITCHELL / WATCH & CLOCK / MAKERS / ABERDEEN. Bdr. with perpetual calendar and regulating instructions. The ptns. were James T. bur. at St. Peters Chyd., Spittal, 30.7.1819; and James M., bur. there 22.8.1850.

TORRY, ALEXANDER. C & WM, Banchory Ternan, KCD, 1837-75. Served his appr. with GEORGE BOOTH, in Aberdeen, and commenced business in 1837. He was an elder of Strachan FC., and walked there every Sunday. This may explain why he erected a well south of the Dee, on the road to Strachan. He d. in reduced circumstances at Stonehaven, 27.11.1883, aged 71.

TROUP, ALEXANDER. CM in Aberdeen, ca. 1790.

WALKER, A.H. Ellon, ABD, 1870-88. Wpr.- A.E. WALKER / WATCHMAKER / & JEWELLER / ELLON. Str. & bkl. bdr., with advert for repairs.

WALKER, GEORGE. CM, Aberdeen, 1685-1720. He was adm. freeman of the Inc. of Hmm. there, 1685, and was deacon of the craft in 1720.

WALKER, JAMES. At 10 Queen Street, Aberdeen, 1847; 48 Broad Street, 1849; 29 St. Nicholas Street, 1850-51; 59 Union Street, before 1862, and at No.135 by 1875, when he ret. Wpr.- Rural scene, with plaque in the centre lettered JAS. WALKER / WATCH & CLOCK MAKER / 29 St. NICHOLAS STREET / ABERDEEN. Fml. bdr. with on lower edge: 'Jewellery sold and repaired'. He was s/o George W., plasterer, and Isabella Milne, and d. unm. at 68 Holburn Street, 14.1.1882. He was bur. in St. Nicholas Chyd.

WALKER, JAMES. Appr. to JOHN MACKIE, C & WM, Ellon, ABD, 1835, and worked for several years as a jour. Succ. his old master at Ellon, 1849. He was Inspector of the Poor at Ellon for about 50 years. James m. Margaret Rennie. Chrn. incl. : 1. George, 1844-1913, d. at Leeds; 2. Elizabeth, 1845-1912; 3. James, 1847-1913. The craftsman prob. ret. ca. 1902, and he d. 10.3.1912, aged 92 years. He was bur. at Allenvale.

WALKER, JAMES. At Old Meldrum, ABD, Mid and Late Victorian periods. Wpr.- JAMES WALKER / WATCH / & CLOCK MAKER / SUPERIOR NEW AND SECOND WATCHES / AT GREATLY REDUCED PRICES / WELL WORTH THE ATTENTION OF THE LABOURING CLASSES / OLD MELDRUM. Narrow bdr. with advert for clocks, barometers, thermometers and wedding rings. James d. 19.5.1893, aged 75 years.

WALKER, JAMES. WM & J, Inverurie, ABD, Mid Victorian period. He d. 14.1.1882, aged 75 years. His sister Isabella, wife of Charles Tait, Inverurie, and George Walker, a gr-neph., were served heirs portioners, 15.11.1882.

WALKER, JAMES. At Dufftown, BAN, Mid Victorian period. Wpr.- JA^S. WALKER / WATCH MAKER / & JEWELLER / FIFE STREET / DUFFTOWN. Fml. quadripartite bdr., inner band lettered: 'Watches & jewellery of every description carefully repaired.' On the back: "25/8/87".

WALLACE, WILLIAM. CR, Aberdeen, 1533. The Town Council app. him "to reulle, set, gid, and keip thair knok of the tolbuith" for 4 merks yearly from 4.4.1533, and he obliged himself "to mend the said knok, and mak her sufficient, and als sufficient, as ony man in Scotland can mak hir".

WALTERS, J. & W. C & WM, Aberdeen, ca. 1820-25.

WANHAGEN, PATRICK. CK, Aberdeen. On 3.9.1651, along with WILLIAM COOK, he was app. "for reuling of the kirk and tolbuith cloak, and to the ringing of the councell bell weiklie on Wednesday, and the said tolbuith and kirk bell on preaching and lecter dayes, and to the ringing of the fyve hour bell in the morning and nyne hour bell at evening", all for payment of 132 merks yearly.

WARDEN, ROBERT. CM in Aberdeen, ca. 1815-20. He had as ptn. for a time, ALEXANDER SIM. Robert made longcase clocks signed "Rt. WARDEN". He may have been related to John W., resident in the town, who prepared manuscripts for the press, and acted as an executor of private writings.

WATSON, JAMES. C & WM, 189 George Street, Aberdeen, 1849-50, when he applied for *cessio bonorum*. He recovered from financial embarrassment, and was at 25 St. Nicholas Street to 1870, when he moved to 81 Union Street. Became James Watson & Son, ca. 1885, and at 113 Union Street, 1895-1900+.

WATSON, WILLIAM. Maryfield, Fyvie, ABD, 1871-1900+. He was a miller with his father at Mill of Towie before commencing business as a C & WM. Moved from North Lodge, Fyvie, to Maryfield. He wound clocks for the Forbes family at Fyvie Castle on a weekly basis: a task performed by the craftsman who succ. him until 1964. William m. Eliza, 1844-1921, d/o Andrew Low, butler. Chrn. incl.: 1. WILLIAM, Jr.; 2. John, who emigrated to Canada, then to USA; 3. Andrew, WM in Canada; 4. Mrs Alexander Sim, emigrated to Boston, MA, USA; 5. Mary, who m. JOHN HUTCHEON, WM. William d. 1919, aged 77 years.

WATSON, WILLIAM, Jr. Rotheienorman, ABD, 1900, later in Stonehaven, KCD. Wpr.- WM. WATSON / WATCHMAKER / AND / JEWELLER / ROTHIENORMAN. Str. & bkl. bdr., with advert for repairs. He was s/o the above WILLIAM W, and m. in 1900, Christina, sist/o JOHN HUTCHEON.

WATSON, -----. C & WM, 82 Union Street, Aberdeen, 1849-50. Ptn., FILLAN & Watson.

WATT, ALEXANDER. Adm. to the Inc. of Hmm. of Aberdeen, 6.11.1883, and as a Trade-B, 3.12.1883. Commenced business as WM & J, at 33 Broad Street in 1890; 576 George Street, 1891-99, and later at Skene Terrace. He resided at 576 George Street, and later moved to Insch. Alexander was s/o GEORGE W. and Jane McGillivray. He d. unm. at 52 Market Street, Inverurie, 3.9. 1916, aged 52 years.

WATT, ARCHIBALD. Appr. to JOHN FRASER, Aberdeen, and after working for a time as a jour., commenced business as C & WM at 128 Gallowgate, in 1853. Moved to No.154 in 1863, and to No. 123½ in 1868. He went to Lumphanan in 1872, and then to Gilcomston Steps, Aberdeen. He ret. ca. 1887, and lived in Gallowgate. His hobby was sacred music, and he was precentor in Gallowgate FC. Archibald was b. in Aberdeen, 25.5.1826, s/o Archibald W., carter, and Margaret Donald. He m. Jane Smith, who d. 20.5.1898. Their son Archibald, Jr. , was choirmaster in Gallowgate in Gallowgate FC, and his family were also musical.

WATT, GEORGE. WM & J, Correction Wynd, Aberdeen, 1860-69. He m. Jane McGillivray, who d. 13.10.1888, aged 65 years. George d. 24.6.1869, aged 52 years. They were the parents of ALEXANDER WATT.

WATT, J. W. WM & J, 27 North Street, Aberdeen, 1886.

WATT, JOHN. Huntly, ABD, ca. Late Victorian period. Wpr.- JOHN WATT / WATCHMAKER / AND / JEWELLER / 7 DUKE STREET / HUNTLY. Fml. bdr.

WATTS, HENRY WILLIAM MAITLAND. WM & J, 82 George Street, Aberdeen, 1888. At No.124, 1889. He d. at 1 Lemon Street, 4.7.1892, s/o Mary Ann Maitland, who m. David Watts, builder.

WEBSTER, JOHN. Trained as a C & WM in Peterhead, and went to Edinburgh to work as a jour. Commenced business at West Port, 1826.

WILL, ALEXANDER. Appr. to JOHN GARTLY, CM in Aberdeen, for 6 years from 16.4.1794. He was afterwards in business at Huntly, and in 1804-5 was a 2nd Lieut.in the Strathbogie Volunteers. He d. before 12.10.1822, when his niece, Catherine Will, in Hexham, Northumberland, was served heir portioner of conquest general to him.

WILL, THOMAS. C & WM, Ellon, ABD, ca. 1820-47.

WILL, THOMAS. At 65 The Square, Huntly, ABD, 1857-77. Wpr.- THO^S. WILL / WATCH / AND / CLOCK MAKER / HUNTLY / WEDDING RINGS. Str. & bkl. bdr., with advert for watches.

WILL, WILLIAM. C & WM, St. Fergus, ABD. He went to Pitburn, in the same parish, where his father lived, and took up farming. The *County Directory of Scotland* shows him there in 1875.

WILLIAMS, S. CM in Aberdeen, 1809.

WILLIAMSON, WILLIAM. CK, adm. B of Banff, 1626.

WILLOX, ALEXANDER. Wright & CK, Aberdeen, 1632.

WILLS, C.F. Peterhead, ABD, ca. 1889-95. Wpr.- C.F. WILLS / WATCHMAKER / AND JEWELLER / 43 / MARISCHAL STREET / PETERHEAD. Double str. & bkl. Bdr., inner advertising repairs.

WILSON, ALEXANDER. Ellon, ABD, ca, 1845. Wpr.- ALEX, WILSON / WATCHMAKER / & JEWELLER / STATION ROAD / ELLON. Orn. bdr.

WILSON, JAMES. C & WM at Loop, Turriff, ABD, before 1800 to about 1830. He was s/o WILLIAM W., CM, Fyvie, and Isobel Robertson, and d. at Maryfield, Fyvie, 29.12.1846, aged 87 years.

WILSON, P. C & WM, Keith, BAN, 1846.

WILSON, P. & SON. Keith, BAN, Mid and Late Victorian periods. The above and a son. Wpr.- P. WILSON & SON / WATCH MAKERS / & JEWELLERS / MID STREET / KEITH. Bdr. has advert for watches, clocks and jewellery. On the back: "24.8.96". Firm still in business 1915.

WILSON, PETER. Dufftown, BAN, ca. 1850. Wpr.- P. WILSON / WATCH & CLOCK MAKER / DUFFTOWN. Orn. bdr., with circlet lettered: BAROMETERS & JEWELLERY REPAIRED.

WILSON, WILLIAM. C & WM, Fyvie, ABD, 1740-80. His brass faced longcase clocks were signed "Wil. Wilson, Loop". He m. Isobel Robertson, 1730-66, with issue: 1. JAMES, C & WM; 2. William; 3. Thomas; 4. Isobel. William d. 14.7.1789, aged 89 years.

WILSON, WILLIAM. Loup, Turriff, ABD, ca. 1830. Poss. s/o the above.

WOOD, JAMES. WM in Aberdeen, 1854, poss. jour., had a son John, aged 10 months, bur. 28.2.1854.

WOOD, JOHN. A blacksmith at Broomhead, Durris, KCD, 1826-60, who became a skilled repairer of clocks, and actually copied a few. He m. Ann Ross, who d. 16.7.1866, aged 77 years. John, whose family is said to have come from Brechin, d. at Stonehaven, 19.6.1866, aged 78 years.

WOOD, JOHN. WM & J, 16 Hadden Street, Aberdeen, 1877. Moved before 1895 to 4 Skene Street.

WOOD, JOHN. Banff, Late Victorian period. Wpr.- JOHN WOOD / WATCHMAKER & JEWELLER / 2 LOW STREET / BANFF. Plain str. & bkl. bdr.

WOOD, JOHN E. WM & J, 3 Longate, Peterhead, ABD, 1877.

WOOD & Co. Aberlour, BAN, Late Victorian period. Wpr.- WOOD & Co. / WATCH & CLOCKMAKERS / JEWELLERS & OPTICIANS / ABERLOUR / [Masonic emblems] WATCHES & JEWELLERY OF EVERY DESCRIPTION CAREFULLY

REPAIRED. Bdr. with advert for silver and plated goods, clocks, watches, barometers and cutlery. On the back: "9.4. 1902".

WUNDERLY, PAUL. German CM, sometime ptn. of AUGUSTE AUER at 42 George Street, Aberdeen, but dissolved by 1872, and continued alone until at least until 1888. He was a native of Scharzwata, Germany, and d. 28.2.1874. By his wife, Sophia, had issue, some of whom d. in his lifetime.

Y

YOUNG, ALEXANDER D. Turriff, ABD, Mid Victorian period. Wpr.- ALEX. D. YOUNG / WATCHMAKER, JEWELLER / AND / OPTICIAN / 37 HIGH STREET / TURRIFF. Str. & bkl. bdr. , with advert for repairs.

YULE, ROBERT. WM & J, 7 Correction Wynd, Aberdeen, 1877-1900+.

Z

ZAMEK, -----. Ptn., Zamek & EDELSHAIN, C & WM, 32-36 Bridge Street, Aberdeen, 1885-90.

ADDENDA

AUER, AUGUSTE. Ptn. of PAUL WUNDERLY, German CM, Aberdeen.
EDELSHAIN, -----. Ptn., ZAMEK & Edelshain, C & WM, Aberdeen.
GORDON, THOMAS. CM & gunsmith, Aberdeen, 1591-99.
KEMP, JAMES. Appr. to DAVID THEMAN, CM & EG, Aberdeen, 1457.

PERIODS

Occasionally in this work, reference has been made to different time periods, well understood by horologists. For the uninitiated these are explained here:

Mid Georgian	1766-1790
Late Georgian	1790-1810
Early Regency	1810-1820
Mid Regency	1820-1830
Late Regency	1830-1837
Early Victorian	1837-1857
Mid Victorian	1857-1877
Late Victorian	1877-1901

PRINCIPAL SOURCES

ABERDEEN. *Aberdeen Journal: Notes & Queries.* Printed vols. in the main libraries.

ABERDEEN. *Aberdeen Register of Indentures,* 1622-1796, printed in *Notes & Queries,* 1st and 2nd series. Reproduced in alphabetical sequence as *Roll of Apprentices: Burgh of Aberdeen,* in three parts, edited by Francis McDonnell. Aberdeen: Aberdeen & North-East Scotland Family History Society, 1994.

ABERDEEN. *Aberdeen Street Directories,* from 1824-1900. Complete run in the Local History Department, Central Library, Rosemount Viaduct, Aberdeen.

ANDERSON, P.J. *Fasti Academiae Mariscallanae Aberdonensis.* 3 vols. Aberdeen: New Spalding Club, 1889-98.

ANDERSON, WILLIAM. *The Scottish Nation.* 3 vols. Edinburgh & London: A. Fullerton & Co., 1878-80.

CENSUS OF SCOTLAND. *Decennial Returns,* 1841-91. In the custody of the Registrar General for Scotland, New Register House, Edinburgh.

DALLAS, ALEXANDER. 'Collection of Watchpapers' preserved by him, and formerly owned by Miss Irene Dallas, Inverness (who provided xerox copies). The originals were purchased at auction in 1982 by David M. Penney, Groom's Cottage, Elsenham Hall, Elsenham, Herts., who provided improved copies.

DOUGLAS, Sir ROBERT. *The Baronage of Scotland.* Edinburgh, 1794.

HUDSON, FELIX. *Scottish Clockmakers: A History to 1900.* Dunfermline, 1984.

HUDSON, FELIX. 'Scottish Painted Dials, 1780-1870', in *Antiquarian Horology,* Winter, 1976 - Autumn, 1977. Reproduced along with 'Some Scottish Longcases' , and 'Longcase Engraved Dials'. London: Antiquarian Horological Society (Monograph 22), 1981.

LAWRANCE, R. MURDOCH. 'Notes on Old Clockmakers', in the *Aberdeen Journal,* 1921-22.

MACLEOD, JOHN. *Index to the Register of Testaments: Commissariot of Aberdeen, 1715-1800.* Edinburgh: Scottish Record Society, 1899.

MUNRO, A.M. *Records of Old Aberdeen.* 2 vols. Aberdeen: Spalding Club, 1898-99.

PERSONAL ESTATES. *Index to the Inventories of Defuncts in the Commissary Books of Aberdeen, Kincardine, Banff, Elgin & Nairn, Inverness, Ross & Cromarty, Sutherland, Caithness, Orkney & Shetland, 1846-67.* Edinburgh: H. M. Stationery Office, 1869.

SCOTLAND. *Indexes to the Services of Heirs in Scotland.* Series begins in 1860. Full set in the National Archives of Scotland, and in the main libraries.

SCOTLAND. *Abridged Register of Sasines,* printed from 1781. National Archives of Scotland.

SCOTLAND. *Gifts and Deposits Series.* National Archives of Scotland.

SCOTLAND. *Northern Notes & Queries,* or *The Scottish Antiquary.* 17 vols. Edited by Rev. A.W.C. Hallen. Edinburgh, 1886-1902.

SCOTLAND. *Scottish Notes & Queries.* In three series, 1888-1935.

SCOTLAND. *Old Parochial Registers of Scotland*, in the custody of the Registrar General for Scotland, New Register House, Edinburgh.

SCOTLAND. *The Scottish Genealogist*, quarterly journal of the Scottish Genealogy Society, 15 Victoria Terrace, Edinburgh.

SCOTT, Rev. HEW. *Fasti Ecclesiae Scoticanae.* New edn., Edinburgh: Oliver & Boyd, vols. 1-8, 1915-1950.

SMITH, JOHN. *Old Scottish Clockmakers, 1453-1850.* 2nd edn., Edinburgh: Oliver & Boyd, 1921.

STUART, JOHN (Ed.). *Extracts from the Council Register of the Burgh of Aberdeen, 1398-1625.* 2 vols. Aberdeen: Spalding Club, 1844-48.

STUART, JOHN (Ed.). *Extracts from the Council Register of the Burgh of Aberdeen, 1625-1747.* 2 vols. Edinburgh: Burgh Records Society, 1872.

WHYTE, DONALD. *Scottish Clock & Watchmakers, 1453-1900.* Edinburgh: Scottish Genealogy Society, 1996.

ABBREVIATIONS

adm.	admitted
app.	appointed, appointment
appr.	apprentice, apprenticed
b.	born
bapt.	baptised
B	Burgess
bdr.	border
bkl.	buckle
bro/o	brother of
bur.	buried
C	Clock
ca.	*circa*, or about
chrn.	children
Chyd.	Churchyard
CK	Clock-keeper
CM	Clock-maker
contr.	contract or contracted
CPM	Compass maker
CR	Clock repairer
CRM	Chronometer maker
d.	died, dead, death
dec.	deceased
d/o	daughter of
d.inf.	died in infancy
DM	Dial maker
dy	died young
EG	Engraver
estab.	establish
FC	Free Church
fml.	formal
FRS	Fellow, Royal Society
G	Guild-brother
GLS	Goldsmith
Gr-son	grandson
Gr-neph	grand-nephew
Hmm.	Hammermen
Inc.	Incorporation
Incl.	Including, included
J	Jeweller
jour.	journeyman
Jr.	Junior
manf.	manufacturer, manufactured
m.	married
nr.	near
NIM	Nautical instrument maker
OP	Optician
orn.	ornate
poss.	possibly
prob.	probably

ptn.	partner, partnership.
ret.	retired
sist/o	sister of
s/o	son of
Sr.	Senior
SS	Silversmith
str.	strap
succ.	succeeded
unm.	unmarried
W	Watch
WCM	Watch case maker
WGM	Watch glass maker
WM	Watch maker
Ws.	Wholesale, wholesaler.

SCOTTISH COUNTY ABBREVIATIONS

Suffix shire only used where there is or was a county town of the name.

ABD	Aberdeenshire	LKS	Lanarkshire
ANS	Angus	MLN	Mid Lothian
ARL	Argyll	MOR	Morayshire
AYR	Ayrshire	NAI	Nairnshire
BAN	Banffshire	OKI	Orkney Islands
BEW	Berwickshire	PEE	Peeblesshire
BUT	Bute	PER	Perthshire
CAI	Caithness	RFW	Renfrewshire
CLK	Clackmannanshire	ROC	Ross and Cromarty
DFS	Dumfriesshire	ROX	Roxburghshire
DNB	Dunbartonshire	SEL	Selkirkshire
ELN	East Lothian	SRI	Shetland Isles
FIF	Fife	STI	Stirlingshire
INV	Inverness-shire	SUT	Sutherland
KCD	Kincardineshire	WIG	Wigtownshire
KRS	Kinross-shire	WLN	West Lothian
KKD	Kirkcudbrightshire		

In returning his best thanks to his Friends for the liberal share of patronage he has enjoyed since he commenced Business in 1830, begs to announce his removal from Castle Street, to those Central premises № 88 Union Street, where the business will be continued in all its branches, including that of Working Optician.

Grateful for past favors J. B. takes leave to assure his friends and Customers that no effort will be wanting on his part to merit their continuance.

His stock of Goods will be found to be New and complete; and equal to any in the first houses in London. They have been purchased by himself in the best markets, and parties may rely upon being well served with superior articles at moderate prices.

88, Union Street,
Aberdeen, 1st June, 1853.